Learning to Study the Bible

LEARNING TO STUDY THE Bible

EARL P. McQUAY

BROADMAN PRESS
NASHVILLE, TENNESSEE

© Copyright 1992 • Broadman Press

All rights reserved

4281-59

ISBN: 0-8054-8159-1

Dewey Decimal Classification: 220.7

Subject Heading: BIBLE — STUDY

Library of Congress Catalog Card Number: 91-31653

Printed in the United States of America

Unless otherwise indicated, Scripture taken from the *New American Standard Bible,* © 1960, 1962, 1963, 1968, 1971, 1972, 1973, 1975, 1977 by The Lockman Foundation. Used by permission. Scripture marked NIV is from the Holy Bible, *New International Version*, copyright © 1973, 1978, 1984 by International Bible Society. Used by permission.

Library of Congress Cataloging-in-Publication Data

McQuay, Earl P.

    Learning to study the Bible / Earl P. McQuay.

       p.   cm.

    Includes bibliographical references.

    ISBN 0-8054-8159-1

    1. Bible—Study. I. Title.

BS600.2.M26 1992   91-31653

220'.07—dc20   CIP

To Frances,
my dear sister
and lifelong friend

Introduction

Discover the joy of delving into the Word of God and studying it for yourself. This book is designed to assist you in Bible study that is interesting, understandable, and practical for you.

The living Creator has spoken. The Sovereign Lord of the universe has revealed Himself in print. "See to it that you do not refuse him who speaks" (Heb. 12:25, NIV). As Paul admonished, "Do your best to present yourself to God as one approved, a workman who does not need to be ashamed and who correctly handles the word of truth" (2 Tim. 2:15, NIV).

Too many Christians find Bible study drudgery. Are Christians *supposed* to enjoy the Bible? Here is the witness of the psalmist: "Your statutes are my heritage forever; / they are the joy of my heart" (Ps. 119:111, NIV). Bible study can be fun, highly profitable, and intensely interesting.

Many give up on Bible study because the task appears to be overwhelming and complicated. Do not throw up your hands in despair, concluding that the Bible is too difficult and complex for you to understand. Do not miss one of the greatest joys of being a Christian—to be blessed, instructed, and guided by the understanding and application of the holy Scriptures. Half the solution is in having a method—in knowing how. That is the reason for this book.

This study guide presents a helpful procedure that employs the principles basic to effective Bible study. The various methods of Bible study are described and applied in a guide to the study of the Book of Philippians. Guidelines for a thorough study of a Bible book are spelled out, covering background, synthesis, and analysis. Various "tools" (types of books that aid Bible study) are identified, and their use is explained.

Using this book as a model for your Bible study in the years to come will improve your understanding of God's Word. Each time you study a new passage, you will find yourself more satisfied with your ability to interpret the Bible. Learning to study the Bible is hard work. It is also rewarding work.

Table of Contents

Part I: Basic Methods of Bible Study

Part II: Tools for Bible Study

Part III: Introduction to a Book Study

Part IV: Analytical Study of a Book

Appendixes

PART I

BASIC METHODS OF BIBLE STUDY

1
Search the Scriptures

One way in which the Bible differs with other books is that you must personally know its Author to master its deeper secrets. It resembles other books in that it must be studied to be understood. Jesus declared, "Search the Scriptures, because you think that in them you have eternal life; and it is these that bear witness of Me" (John 5:39). The Greek word for "search" that Jesus used is defined by Charles Spurgeon as "a strict, close, diligent, curious search, such as men make when they are seeking gold, or hunters when they are in earnest after game."

A few years ago three teenagers discovered an eighty-five-ounce gold nugget in an abandoned gold digging area of Wedderburn, Australia. Their find precipitated a flood of gold hunters in the area who were anxious to make it rich. Sometimes in Bible study we assume that we have mined all the riches present in a passage. However, some time later we discover, to our amazement, more riches than we ever imagined! The reason is that the Bible is God's inexhaustible mine of truth.

More gold always lies in the Word of God, waiting to be discovered by the searching student. Grace Noll Crowell wrote of the search as follows:

> I open it, my fingers trace the lines
> That Wesley's, Moody's, Spurgeon's eyes have scanned.
>> Beneath my fingertips a promise shines:
> A diamond unearthed by my seeking hand:
>> A gem that countless saints have touched before
>> And left among this jewel casket's store.
>
> I search as one who searches long for gold,
> And oh, what gleaming nuggets I unearth.
>> All that my seeking heart and hands can hold
> I gather, and I know their precious worth,
>> And strange, the vein has never failed, though men
>> Have mined its channels since the world began.

This manual is a study of the various methods of Bible study and application of the methods in a study of the Book of Philippians. Following a general coverage of the methods of Bible study, you will be directed in a personal study of the background and synthesis of Philippians. Philippians then will be divided into eleven segments. For each segment you will engage in an analytical study covering text/translations, diagram (and outline or paraphrase), observations, cross-references, commentaries, and topical/word studies.

The aim of this guide is to introduce a helpful procedure that employs the principles that are basic to effective Bible study. Because of the complex nature of human thought processes, no one can dictate a precise and rigid formula for Bible study that everyone should follow. This guide is intended to:

a. acquaint you with the different *methods* of Bible study;
b. guide you in applying the various methods in an *example book study* in the Book of Philippians; and
c. assist you in the study of the Bible *on your own*.

To whet your appetite for Bible study, look up the following Scripture verses that reveal the value of Bible study, and fill in the blanks.

A. *The Bible is* described in 2 Timothy 3:15-17 as:

1. A _____-centered book
2. A _____-saving book
3. A _____-inspired book
4. A _____-perfecting book

B. The *value* of studying the Bible is understood when one comprehends the purposes that the Word of God fulfills in the human life. A number of figures of speech are used in the Word to illustrate its significance. Look up each of the following verses and note the imagery used and the personal application.

1. James 1:23,24—The Bible is a *mirror* that *convicts* me of sin, reveals my true condition, and shows me what change is needed.

2. Jeremiah 23:29—

3. Ephesians 5:26—

4. Deuteronomy 8:3; Psalm 19:10; Hebrews 5:12,14—

5. Psalm 119:105—

6. Ephesians 6:16-17—

7. Psalm 119:72—

8. Luke 8:5,11—

C. The *prerequisites* (three *D*'s) for Bible study are:

1. *D*_____ (Jas. 4:8; Matt. 5:6);

2. *D*_____ upon the Holy Spirit (John 14:26; 1 Cor. 2:11-13); and

3. *D*_____ in applying oneself to the study of the Word (2 Tim. 2:15).

You will find answers to the questions in the back of the book.

2
Six Methods of Bible Study

Students of Scripture have identified as many as twenty-five Bible study methods or approaches one may use in studying the Scriptures. We can boil down the approaches to the following six basic methods.

Critical Method

The critical method deals with the scientific investigation of the scriptural documents to determine their origin, original form, history, and purpose. "Biblical criticism" deals with questions concerning the inspiration and preservation of the text.

Criticism and *introduction* are related terms in Bible study. Many books that treat the critical questions of Scripture include the word *introduction* in their titles (examples: Roland K. Harrison, *An Introduction to the Old Testament* and Donald Guthrie, *New Testament Introduction*).

Two divisions of Bible introduction are *general introduction* and *special introduction*. General introduction deals with general questions about the integrity of the Bible, such as inspiration, authority, canon, languages, text, genuineness, authenticity, and credibility.

Consult two appendixes to get an overview of the issues of general introduction. Appendix C, "How We Got God's Word," deals with revelation, inspiration, canonicity, preservation, and illumination. Appendix D, "Variations in the Transmitted Text," presents an example of how one can deal with the problem of textual variations in the many copies of the Scripture that are extant.

Special introduction takes up where general introduction leaves off and deals with questions concerning the characteristics of the Bible books, such as author, destination, date, origin, occasion, unity, design, and peculiarities.

Biographical Method

Magazines filled with pictures and articles about people have a large circulation. Why? Because people are interested in people. The message of the Bible is interwoven with the lives of people. The Bible, therefore, has high reader appeal.

The biographical method involves the study of a particular person in the Bible in order to see the facts of his or her life and the lessons from that life. We profit from studying the personalities of the Scripture because the Bible was written *about* people and *for* people. Paul brought up both of these facts in his statement, "Now these things happened to them as an example, and they were written for our instruction, upon whom the ends of the ages have come" (1 Cor. 10:11).

Roy Laurin has said, "The Bible presents the answers to our personal problems not only in lofty principles but also in the experiences of the men and women who make up its cast of characters."[1] James reveals why we enjoy studying the life of a man like Elijah and why we profit from such a study: "Elijah was a man with a nature like ours" (Jas. 5:17).

Historical—Geographical Method

The Bible was written in another time and place. Unless we know the setting of a biblical passage, we will interpret it according to our present-day setting in our own culture. We understand the Bible better when we consider its message in the light of its original setting.

Every biblical event and teaching arose from and is a part of a particular history and culture. The writer selected factors in the life of an individual, group, or nation to give meaning to the acts and purposes of his subject. Most portions of Scripture are more readily understood when we set them against their own historical and cultural situations. Then we can understand why people thought and acted as they did, and we are ready to understand the meaning of the events and teachings for our day.

The historical-geographical method of Bible study aims to discover the time-place setting of the Word. This method covers the following aspects of the biblical scene: history (social, religious, political, and military), chronology (dates and order of events), archaeology (uncovering of the buildings and implements of ancient life), geography (land, cities, bodies of water, mountains, animals, and climate), and customs (food, dress, habits, outlook on life, economy, transportation, building materials, tools, writing materials, institutions, arts, music, and national and international relations).

Synthetical Method

Medical students begin their studies of anatomy by mastering the construction of the human skeleton. In similar principle, Bible students begin their study of the Bible by understanding its skeletal framework.

The synthetical method deals with the general content of the Bible or an individual Bible book. The word *synthesis* means "putting together," and in Bible study it involves a "bird's eye" view. This synthetical study aims to understand the "big picture,"—that is, the overall, progressive plan, or the connecting story thread.

Items considered in a synthesis are the theme (with key verses and words), development and outline of each book, and its relation to other books of the Bible.

Analytical Method

The analytical method is an extensive, detailed study of a particular Bible book or passage. *Synthesis* and *analysis* are antonyms. *Analysis* means "breaking up into parts." The analytical method of Bible study breaks a book or passage into small parts and makes a "snail's eye" investigation of it.

Phases of study in Bible analysis are: text/translations, outline (with diagram and paraphrase), detailed observations, cross-references, commentaries, and word studies. The analytical study involves what Irving L. Jensen calls "charting a chapter," "probing a paragraph," "examining a verse," "weighing a word," and "organizing a topic."[2]

Topical/Word Study Method

The topical/word study method involves an extensive study of a particular word, topic, or doctrine in Scripture. *Topical study* (study of a general theme that may involve one word or several related words) and *word study* (study of one specific biblical word) are closely related. A word study concentrates on one specific word, such as *reconciliation*. A topical study could deal with a general theme, such as the final rewards for the Christian, which would involve studying related words likes *rewards, crowns, the judgment seat of Christ,* and *promises for faithfulness.* Three steps involved in a topical or word study are research, summary, and conclusion.

Implementation of the Six Methods

Two basic types of Bible study are Bible surveys and book studies. The Bible survey takes a "telescopic" look at the Scriptures. A book study takes a "microscopic" look.

A Bible survey may involve any one or a combination of five of the Bible study methods— critical, biographical, historical-geographical, synthetical, and topical/word study. The only method that would not be involved in a Bible survey is the analytical method since by its very nature it involves the microscopic look at a book.

In a book study all six methods may be employed. The critical, biographical, historical-geographical, and synthetical methods are pursued for background material on the book under study. The analytical method is pursued in making a detailed study of the book. The topical/word study method is pursued for an in-depth understanding of topics and words in the book.

This manual will concentrate on a book study. All six methods will be employed in a study of the Book of Philippians.

Match each of the six methods of Bible study with the most appropriate identifying phrase:

1. Critical—
2. Biographical—
3. Historical-geographical—
4. Synthetical—
5. Analytical—
6. Topical/word study—

A. covers the time-place setting (history, chronology, geography, customs)
B. studies a particular person in order to see the facts and lessons of his or her life
C. breaks up into small parts and makes a detailed study
D. investigates the Scriptural documents to determine their origin, original form, history and purpose
E. deals with the general content (theme, development, outline, relation to other books)
F. extensively researches a particular word or subject

Fill in each blank with the most appropriate word:

7. _____ introduction deals with critical questions about the integrity of the Scriptures.

8. _____ introduction deals with critical questions about the characteristics of the Bible books.

9. _____ involves the uncovering of buildings and implements of ancient life.

10. A _____ study covers a general theme that may involve one word or several words related to a particular subject.

11. Two basic types of Bible study are a _____ _____, which takes a "telescopic" look at the Scriptures, and a _____ _____, which takes a "microscopic" look at an individual book of the Bible.

You will find the answers to the questions in the back of the book.

Notes
1. Roy Laurin, *Meet Yourself in the Bible* (Wheaton, Ill.: Van Kampen Press, 1946), 1.
2. Irving L. Jensen, *Enjoy Your Bible* (Chicago: The Moody Bible Institute, 1978), 57-115.

PART II

TOOLS FOR BIBLE STUDY

3
Tools for Background Study

Many tools are available to the carpenter to enable him to do quality work with wood. A basic part of his apprenticeship is to acquaint himself with the tools and to become adept in using them.

Through the years marvelous tools have been developed to assist Bible students in their study of the Scriptures. There are study Bibles, Bible dictionaries, concordances, and numerous other tools. Chapters 3 and 4 will guide you in becoming acquainted with the Bible study tools and their use.

General

The first group of tools are classified as "general" because they have multiple uses and serve as resources in all methods of Bible study.

Study Bible

Purpose: To provide—along with the Scripture text—book introductions, helpful notes, marginal references, cross-references, a concordance, a topical index, maps, charts, and various other aids. One of the most widely used general Bible study tools.

Marginal notes and footnotes in a study Bible (usually indicated by raised numbers) give an alternate rendering or explain the meaning of the subject. Cross-references (usually indicated by raised letters) indicate other Scripture references that bear on the same subject. A chain-reference system will lead the student from one verse to another through a number of related passages.

Recommendations: Disciple's Study Bible, NIV (Holman); *The New Open Bible,* NASB (Nelson); *Thompson Chain-Reference Bible,* NIV (Kirkbride); *The NIV Study Bible* (Zondervan).

Bible Dictionary/Encyclopedia

A Bible dictionary and encyclopedia are similar. An encyclopedia is more extensive in its coverage.

Purpose: To give a general coverage of all Bible topics (persons, places, things, concepts, words) in alphabetical order with definition and systematic commentary. A vital tool containing a wealth of information valuable to Bible students.

Content: Gives alphabetical listing of biblical terms and subjects with definitions and background material. Has helpful derivations, pronunciation aids, and Bible maps. Provides general coverage of critical, historical, geographical, and topical areas in Bible study.

Use: Look up any subject in its alphabetical position.

Recommendations: Holman Bible Dictionary (Holman); *The New Bible Dictionary* (Eerdmans); *Unger's Bible Dictionary* (Moody); *The Interpreter's Dictionary of the Bible* (Abingdon); *International Standard Bible Encyclopedia* (Eerdmans); *Zondervan Pictorial Encyclopedia* (Zondervan).

Bible Handbook

Purpose: To provide a collection of helpful comments about the Bible and each of its books.

Content: Gives an introduction to each Bible book, an abbreviated (terse chapter-by-chapter) commentary, and a historical and geographical background. Has maps, charts, outlines, diagrams, and illustrations. Provides information about how the Bible came to us, archaeological discoveries, church history, and religions of the world.

Use: Find information on each Bible book in the same order that the book appears in the English Bible or information about the Bible in general.

Recommendations: Unger's Bible Handbook (Moody); *Halley's Bible Handbook* (Zondervan); *Eerdman's Handbook on the Bible* (Eerdmans); *Holman Bible Handbook* (Holman).

Bible Survey

Purpose: To provide a collection of helpful comments about the Bible, as does the Bible handbook, but with less background and more explanation of the spiritual message of each book.

Recommendations: What The Bible Is All About, Henrietta C. Mears (Regal); *Strategic Grasp of the Bible,* J. Sidlow Baxter (Zondervan).

Principles and Methods of Bible Study

The science of interpreting the Bible, known as hermeneutics, has become increasingly important in recent decades. Principles of Bible study will be covered later in this manual. Helpful and reliable tools on the subject are *How to Understand Your Bible,* T. Norton Sterrett (Inter-Varsity); and *Principles of Biblical Interpretation,* L. Berkhof (Baker).

Books similar to this manual deal with methods of Bible study, that is, *how* to study the Bible. Some helpful tools in this area are *Effective Bible Study,* Howard F. Vos (Zondervan); *The Joy of Discovery in Bible Study,* Oletta Wald (Augsburg); and *How to Study Your Bible,* Gordon Talbot (Back to the Bible).

Bible Introduction

Purpose: To treat the critical questions of Scripture. General introduction treats general questions regarding the integrity of the Bible. Special introduction deals with questions concerning the characteristics of the Bible books, such as author, date, occasion, design, and outline.

Recommendations: A *Survey of Old Testament Introduction*, Gleason L. Archer (Moody); *An Introduction to the Old Testament*, R. K. Harrison (Eerdmans); *New Testament Introduction*, Donald Guthrie (Inter-Varsity Press); *Old Testament Survey*, Paul House (Broadman).

A certain amount of introductory information may be obtained from the Bible dictionary or encyclopedia and the Bible handbook.

Setting/Context

The tools in this category help you to step back into the unfamiliar world of the past. They provide biblical background information of the following types: biographical, geographical, historical, and archaeological.

Biblical Character Studies

Purpose: To provide coverage of the personalities of the Bible.

Recommendations: *Bible Characters*, Alexander Whyte (Baker); *Paul, Apostle of the Heart Set Free*, F. F. Bruce (Eerdmans). Information on biblical characters may be obtained also from the Bible dictionary or encyclopedia.

Bible Atlas

Purpose: To orient you as you read about various locations in the Bible and to clarify the dimensions of time and place in the biblical narrative.

Content: Provides a collection of maps showing the lands and location of biblical events and geographical and historical information concerning biblical places, lands, peoples, and things. Gives attention to archaeological discoveries. Has photographs and chronologies.

Use: Use the table of contents and the index to locate the geographical and historical setting of a Bible passage.

Recommendations: *Macmillan Bible Atlas* (Macmillan); *Atlas of the Bible Lands* (Scripture Press); and *Oxford Bible Atlas* (Oxford).

Bible History

Purpose: To enlighten you concerning the historical and cultural backgrounds of the Bible passage.

Content: Provides abundant information concerning the civilization, culture, customs, religious backgrounds, and other details concerning the peoples of biblical history.

Use: Find the chapter(s) of the Bible history book that deals with the time corresponding to the Bible book you are studying. Make use also of the table of contents and the index.

Recommendations: *Historical Backgrounds of Bible History*, J. P. Lewis (Baker); *A Survey of Israel's History*, L. J. Wood (Zondervan); *Old Testament Bible History*, Alfred Edersheim (Eerdmans); *Life and Times of Jesus the Messiah*, Alfred Edersheim (Eerdmans); *New Testament Times*, M. C. Tenney (Eerdmans).

Charts and Chronological Outlines

Purpose: To help locate the historical setting of Bible events and persons. *Chronology* has to do primarily with time or dates.

Recommendations: The Student's Chronological New Testament, A. T. Robertson (Revell); *Chronological and Background Charts of the New Testament,* H. Wayne House (Zondervan).

Archaeology

Purpose: To provide help in confirming scriptural facts and illuminating the Bible student. Note: Archaeological discoveries are not essential to faith in the inspiration of Scripture.

Recommendations: Archaeology and Bible History, Joseph P. Free (Victor); *Archaeology in Bible Lands,* Howard F. Vos (Moody). Information on biblical archaeology may be obtained also from a Bible dictionary or encyclopedia and Bible handbook.

We have named and described the following eleven tools:

1. Study Bible
2. Bible dictionary/encyclopedia
3. Bible handbook
4. Bible survey
5. Bible study methods
6. Bible introduction
7. Biblical character studies
8. Bible atlas
9. Bible history
10. Charts and chronological outlines
11. Archaeology

Write the number of the tool listed above by the description below that best describes it:

____ A. Coverage of personalities of the Bible.

____ B. An introduction to and abbreviated commentary on each Bible book.

____ C. Historical and cultural backgrounds.

____ D. Helpful notes, cross-references, and various other aids along with the Scripture text.

____ E. Treatment of critical questions of Scripture, such as integrity, authorship, occasion, and outline.

More than one of the tools may be consulted for information on each of the following items. In each case, indicate (by numbers) as many tools as are requested.

____ F. Paul, writer of Philippians (list two tools).

____ G. Philippi—historical and/or geographical information (list four tools).

____ H. Outline and message of Philippians (list five tools).

You will find the answers in the back of the book.

4
Tools for In-depth Study

Commentary

Commentaries are indispensable helps to a thorough study of the Bible. A commentary is not the final word in interpreting the Scriptures. Commentators do not always agree with each other. Comparing commentaries will help you solve textual problems, avoid strange and fanciful interpretations of Bible passages, and become a person of conviction as to what the Scriptures say.

Purpose: To present a systematic and detailed explanation or interpretation of the books of the Bible.

Kinds: Some are complete in one volume; others are multi-volumed. Some focus on chapters, some on paragraphs, and others on word-by-word studies. Some are designed for the English-reading student; others are designed for one who has a working knowledge of the original languages. Some are devotional (presenting inspirational applications); others are critical (giving more on background, theology, and language).

Use: Look up the passage of your interest in the same order that it appears in the English Bible.

Suggestion: A one-volume commentary is adequate for general Bible study. Large sets of commentaries are available for detailed study. Acquire a good one-volume commentary on the entire Bible for general and quick reference. Then you may wish to acquire a good multi-volume commentary on the entire Bible. Thereafter, it may be best to acquire commentaries and studies on individual Bible books (or divisions, such as the minor prophets) by the key writers in the particular fields.

Recommendations: The New Bible Commentary (Eerdmans); *The Wycliffe Bible Commentary* (Moody); Series—*New International Commentary* (Eerdmans); *The New American Commentary* (Broadman).

Other tools that may be included in the commentary category are study aids on individual books (such as Irving L. Jensen's study guides), Sunday School teacher's guides and quarterlies, and books of expository sermons. Warren Wiersbe has edited two helpful books of expository sermons: *Listening To the Giants* (Baker) and *Treasury of the World's Great Sermons* (Kregel).

Linguistic

Linguistic tools assist the Bible student in discovering the meaning that the Bible writers had in mind when they wrote their messages in the original languages. Though one may not be a student of Hebrew or Greek, one can take advantage of what others have gained through a study of these languages.

Translation/Paraphrase

A comparison of various Bible translations can help the student to derive an understanding of the meaning of a passage. One translation may have a more understandable way than another of presenting the thoughts of the biblical writer.

Purpose: To present to the present-day mind an up-to-date rendering of the Bible text because language is a constantly changing medium of communication and reflects changes in culture in ways of living, thinking, and expressing ideas.

Use: Compare a passage in several translations to help you find the shade and depth of meaning. Paragraph divisions in some of the translations are helpful in outlining and in identifying the context in order to determine the central teaching of a passage.

Recommendations: New American Standard Bible (Holman); *New International Version* (Holman, Zondervan); *New King James Bible* (Nelson).

Paraphrase: A paraphrase is not a close translation of the original language, but an attempt to put its meaning in language easy to understand. A paraphrase can be excitingly enlightening. *The Living Bible*, by Kenneth Taylor (Tyndale) is the most widely used paraphrase. Another popular one is *The New Testament in Modern English*, by J. B. Phillips (Macmillan).

Word Study

Word study books are specialized treatments of select biblical words and their cognates (derivations, related words).

Purpose: To detail the meanings and uses of Hebrew and Greek words.

Use: Look up the word of your interest in alphabetical order. The words may be treated in alphabetical order, or they may be listed according to the original language. If the latter is the case, probably there will be an English index that you may use.

Recommendations: Expository Dictionary of Old and New Testament Words, W. E. Vine (Revell); *Word Studies in the New Testament*, M. E. Vincent (Eerdmans); *Synonyms of the Old Testament*, R. B. Girdlestone (Eerdmans); *Word Pictures in the New Testament*, A. T. Robertson (Broadman).

Grammars, Interlinear Translations, Lexicons

Hebrew and Greek grammars, interlinear translations, and lexicons assist the Bible student in studying the Bible in the original languages. For one unable to read the original languages, an analytical concordance with transliterations of the original words in Roman script is a help toward a more accurate understanding of the original writing.

Cross-Reference

Concordance

A concordance is one of the most valuable helps to a Bible student.

Purpose: To list all the words in the English Bible alphabetically with references to where the words are used (in order from Gen. to Rev.). A concordance can help locate verses and speed up Bible study. It can also help when developing theme studies on certain subjects.

Kinds: (a) Abbreviated (abridged) lists the major verses, and (b) Analytical (complete, unabridged) lists all the verses where a word appears.

Use: (a) To locate *a verse* in which a certain word appears. Look up the most probable key word. (Example: "In all thy ways acknowledge Him..." The key words are *ways* and *acknowl-*

edge. Locate these words in a concordance and you will find the reference is Prov. 3:6.) (b) To locate a *number of verses* that use a certain word. The number of references will be determined accordingly as the concordance is abridged or unabridged. (c) To trace the *Greek or Hebrew word* to find the shade and depth of meaning by comparing the texts in which it is used. An analytical concordance classifies the verses according to the particular Hebrew or Greek words from which each English word is translated.

Recommendations: Cruden's Concordance—Handy Reference Edition (Baker); *Young's Concordance to the Bible* (Eerdmans); *New American Standard Exhaustive Concordance of the Bible* (Holman).

Cross-Reference Books

Some cross-reference books, such as *Treasury of Scripture Knowledge,* are available. The *Treasury* contains over 500,000 Scripture references and parallel passages arranged in chapter and verse order. In studying a verse of Scripture, all the weight of the entire Bible is brought to bear upon the verse by the cross-reference suggested.

The typical Bible student, however, may find the cross-references provided in a study Bible to be adequate for tracing parallel passages.

Harmonies

Purpose: To show which passages of Scripture are parallel and which are not. The references from different Bible books are arranged in chronological order and parallel columns. This brings together all the details regarding a particular incident.

Recommendations: A Harmony of the Gospels (NASB), Robert L. Thomas and Stanley N. Gundry (Moody); *Harmony of the Life of St. Paul,* Frank J. Goodwin (Baker); *A Harmony of Samuel, Kings, and Chronicles,* William D. Crockett (Baker).

Topical

Topical Bible

A topical Bible, such as *Nave's Topical Bible,* is helpful in topical studies. Whereas a concordance directs the student to Scripture verses that use a specific word, a topical Bible brings together verses that are related to a general topic.

Theology Book

Purpose: To provide a deeper knowledge of the doctrines of the Christian faith that are revealed in the Bible.

Content: Deals with representative Scripture passages that relate to the subject under consideration and formulates the doctrinal teaching in a systematic presentation.

Use: Follow the table of contents and subject index and look up the subject under consideration to find help in understanding. Sometimes a Scripture reference index is provided in the theology book. This is helpful in finding the section where the verses you are studying are treated in the theology book.

Recommendations: Systematic Theology, L. Berkhof (Eerdmans); *Lectures in Systematic Theology,* Henry Thiessen (Eerdmans).

Books on Particular Subjects

Myriads of books have been written that cover a particular Bible subject in an extensive manner. *Angels*, Billy Graham (Pocket Books); *The Atonement*, Archibald A. Hodge (Baker); and *Whatever Happened to Hell?*, Jon Braun (Nelson) are examples. The Bible student should be alert to find and use such books when studying particular subjects in the Scriptures.

An additional ten tools have been named and described in this chapter:

12. Commentary
13. Translation/Paraphrase
14. Word study
15. Grammars, interlinear translations, and lexicons
16. Concordance
17. Cross-reference books
18. Harmonies
19. Topical Bible
20. Theology
21. Books on particular subjects

Write the number of the tool that is best described by each of the descriptions below:

_____ A. List all biblical words alphabetically with references to where the words are used.
_____ B. Presents a systematic and detailed explanation or interpretation of the books of the Bible.
_____ C. References from different Bible books are arranged in chronological order and parallel columns to show which passages are parallel.
_____ D. Specialized treatments of select biblical words and words related to them in the original language.

Which tools may be consulted for information on each of the following items? Indicate (by number) as many tools as are requested:

_____ E. Locate possible ways in which Philippians 1:6 ("will perfect it until the day of Christ Jesus") could be translated in English. (Specify one tool.)
_____ F. Locate other Scripture verses that parallel in thought Philippians 2:9 ("Therefore also God highly exalted Him, and bestowed on Him the name which is above every name"). (List three tools.)
_____ G. How many of the above tools could be helpful to a skilled Bible student in an extensive, in-depth study of three terms used by Paul in Philippians? [See "the day of Christ Jesus" (1:6), "lights in the world" (2:15), and "the peace of God" (4:7).]

You will find the answers to the questions in the back of the book.

Note: See Appendix B, "Bible Study Tools," for a recommended bibliography for students of Scripture, developed by the author in consultation with thirty faculty members of Columbia Bible College and Graduate School.

Additional Suggestions

In your church library, a public library, a Christian friend's library, or a Christian bookstore, examine samples of the twenty-one tools to become better acquainted with them.

Begin to acquire some of the basic Bible study tools for your personal library. Buy slowly, buy carefully, and buy well. Be certain that each book will meet your need and will be one of substance for future use.

Chart: The Bible Study Tools

Two Basic Types of Bible Study:

1. **Survey:** Any one or combination of methods 1-4 and 6 may be pursued.
2. **Book Study:** Methods 1-4 are pursued for *background* material;
   Method 5 involves a *detailed study* of the book itself; and
   Method 6 is pursued for *extension* of thought and increased understanding.

Methods (and areas included):	Tools:	Purchase Priority:
1. Critical (tools: A and B)	**A. General**	
General Introduction: Inspiration, Authority, Canon, Languages, Text, Genuineness, Authenticity, Credibility	1. Study Bible	(1)
Special Introduction (individual books): Author, Destination, Date, Origin, Occasion, Unity, Design, Peculiarities	2. Bible Dictionary, Encyclopedia	(2)
	3. Bible Handbook	(5)
	4. Bible Survey	
	5. Bible Study Methods	
2. Biographical (tools: A and C)	**B. Bible Introduction**	
Study of Bible personalities (both principal and minor)	6. Bible Introduction	
	a. General Introduction	
	b. Special Introduction (OT, NT, and individual books)	
3. Historical-Geographical (tools: A and C)	**C. Setting**	
History, Chronology, Archaeology, Geography, Customs	7. Biblical Character Studies	
	8. Atlas, Biblical Backgrounds	(8)
	9. Bible History	(9)
	10. Charts and Chronological Outlines	
	11. Archaeology	
4. Synthetical (tools: A, B, and D)	**D. Commentary**	
Theme, Development, Outline, Key verse, Key words, Relation to other books	12. Commentaries	(3)
	(Study Aids on Individual books, Books of Expository Sermons, and S.S. Teacher's Guides and Quarterlies)	
5. Analytical (tools: A, D, E, and F)	**E. Linguistic**	
Detailed study by chapter, paragraph, and word	13. Translations/Paraphrase	(6)
	14. Word-Study Books	(10)
	15. Grammars, Interliner Translations, and Lexicons	
6. Topical Word (tools: A, D, E, F, and G)	**F. Cross-Reference**	
Extensive study of themes or words through relative Scripture passages	16. Concordance	(4)
	17. Bible Cross-reference Books (and Bible marginal references)	
	18. Harmonies	
	G. Topical	
	19. Topical Bible	
	20. Theology Works	(7)
	21. Books on Particular Subjects	

PART III

INTRODUCTION TO A BOOK STUDY

5
How to Study a Bible Book

We have stated that all six methods of Bible study may be incorporated in an in-depth study of a Bible book. Let's begin to do this in a study of the Book of Philippians.

God has given us His Word in the form of books: sixty-six all total. After gaining a general overview of the complete Bible, the student should develop his knowledge of the Word by studying individual books. In the remainder of this study guide, you will be guided in a study of Philippians. At the same time you will be aided in developing skills that you will be able to use in all your future studies in Bible books. Are you ready to begin a study of Philippians? On your mark, let's go!

Two Vital Prerequisites

To begin with, you should note two exercises that are vital first steps in the study of Scripture.

Prayer

Because an understanding of the Holy Scriptures is dependent upon the Holy Spirit (1 Cor. 2:9-16), the first act in Bible study should be that of prayer for His guidance and illumination. The methods of study should be pursued in dependence upon Him.

Your special assignment now will be to pause and pray for the Holy Spirit to guide you in your study of Philippians and all your future study of His Word.
- Tell Him that you desire to know His Word and be a life-long student of it.
- Ask Him to be your Teacher and give you guidance and illumination from His Word.
- Request that He open to you the truths of Philippians and apply them to your life.
- Share with Him your concern to develop skills in using the principles and methods of Bible study that will help you to be a diligent Bible student.

Remember that prayer is the number one prerequisite to Bible study and endeavor to establish the habit of praying for the Holy Spirit's guidance and illumination each time you begin to study the Word.

Reading

Strangely enough, some endeavor to become students of the Word by studying books about the Bible and by-passing the most important means of grasping God's Word, that is, by reading the Word itself.

Writing is designed for reading! An interesting title once given to the preface of a book was "To Be Read." That should be placed over the Scriptures as a vital phase of Bible study. The basic method of studying the Bible is to read it. The key to opening a passage to one's mind is contained in the very nature of the writing itself, and the key is reading.

Once I was given a used, but good, suitcase, for which I desired to obtain a key. We had a key made for the lock at a leather shop. Sometime later I discovered a key hidden under a pocket inside the suitcase. I had never known that the key was there in the suitcase itself. The Bible student could have a similar problem in his study of Scripture. The key that opens the Scripture is reading. Only after we have read the Scripture should we endeavor to follow additional methods of probing its depths. We look for fancy methods of understanding the Scriptures and sometimes fail to use the basic method—reading the Word.

At the beginning of the study of a Bible book, acquaint yourself with the book itself. Read it through in one sitting if possible. Read it in several translations. Dr. G. Campbell Morgan, a great English expositor of the Scriptures, said that before expounding a given book of the Bible he would read it through fifty times to get a clear view of the broad sweep of teaching in the book.

Since the reading of the Word is so important, why don't you open your Bible to the Book of Philippians and read its short four chapters in one sitting.

After reading the book, write (in one sentence) the key message of the book as you see it.
Key message: _____

_____

Next, it would be good for you to read through the Book of Philippians in a paraphrase (*The Living Bible; The New Testament in Modern English* by J. B. Phillips; or *The Letters of St. Paul* by A. S. Way). As you read the paraphrase, note several ideas that you did not see in the previous reading.

New ideas seen: _____

_____

_____

Get the Picture!

Imagine that you are standing before a huge painting and you desire to make a thorough study of it. Let's suggest that you divide your study into three phases that will cover: (A) the frame, (B) the overall scene, and (C) the details of the picture.

The steps involved in a study of a Bible book may be classified under the three major aspects illustrated by the viewing of a painting—seeing the frame, viewing the overall scene, and scrutinizing the details of the painting. Everything that should be included in a book study fits under these three phases, as seen in the following outline:

The three phases	The six methods	The study details
A. The Frame	Critical	Author, destination, date, origin, occasion, peculiarities
	Biographical	Study of the persons associated with or included in the book
	Historical/ Geographical	History, chronology, archaeology, geography, customs
B. The Overall Scene	Synthetical	Theme, key verse, key words, development, relation to other books, outline
C. The Detail Study	Analytical	Text/translation, diagram/outline/ paraphrase, observations, cross-references, commentaries
	Topical/Word	Extensive study of particular topics or words

To help you see a little more clearly the general idea of each of the three phases, consider the following:

A. The Frame

Before you get into the study of the content of the book, you should gain some background information about the book. Answer *critical* questions such as: Who wrote it? When? From where? To whom? Why? Answer *biographical* questions such as: What do we know about the author's life and character? What do we know about persons named in the book? Answer *historical-geographical* questions such as: What were the place and people like about whom the book was written? Where does the book fit chronologically in history and theologically in God's plan of redemption?

B. The Overall Scene

Move from the frame to the picture itself. First discern the overall scene. Take a look at the general content of the book. Answer the *synthetical* questions: What is its theme, key verse, key words, development of idea, relation to other books, and book outline?

C. The Detail Study

Once you have the frame and overall scene clearly in mind, you are ready to take the "snail's eye view" of the book in an *analytical* study. Take one segment (about ten to fifteen verses or a paragraph) at a time and investigate it thoroughly. Get all that you can for yourself through a comparison of translations, the composition of your own diagram, outline, or paraphrase of the segment, and your own careful observations. The next step will be to compare the passage with other Scriptures through cross-references. Then check your findings with other writers by consulting their commentaries. Finally, you may need to use the *topical/word* method to make an extensive study of particular topics or words that derive from the passage.

By each phase of a Bible book study (A, B, and C), write the numbers of all the areas that would be included under the phase.

A. The Frame   _____

B. The Overall Scene   _____

C. The Detail Study   _____

    1. Theme of the book   7. One segment at a time
    2. Analytical study   8. Biographical questions
    3. Background information   9. Topical/Word study
    4. Why the book was written   10. Where the book fits chronologically
    5. Key words in the book   11. Diagram of the segment
    6. Relation to other books   12. Outline of the book

You will find the answers to the questions in the back of the book.

6
Background of Philippians

When beginning a book study, gather information about the background of the book. We have indicated that three methods are incorporated in a study of the background of a Bible book—the critical, biographical, and historical methods. These compose *the frame* of the picture (see chap. 5).

FRAME

BIOGRAPHICAL

CRITICAL

GEOGRAPHICAL

HISTORICAL —

In any phase of Bible study you should endeavor to get as much as you can from a direct study of the Bible book itself before consulting other books such as commentaries. After you have gotten what you can for yourself, then you will want to consult the Bible study tools. Follow this principle in each of the following steps in the study of the background of Philippians.

Note: The procedure outlined in the remainder of this book is intended to serve as a guide to you in your future study of *any* Bible book. The questions are comprehensive and not all will necessarily apply in every Bible book study.

Critical Background

"Special introduction" deals with individual books of the Bible and covers the following designated critical questions.

First, search through the Book of Philippians for answers to the questions. Get as much as you can from the book itself before consulting the tools for additional answers.

Second, consult at least one (preferably three) Bible study tool for additional answers.

TOOLS for background:
- Study Bible
- Bible Dictionary, Encyclopedia
- Bible Handbook
- Bible Survey
- Bible Introduction
- Biblical character studies
- Atlas, Biblical backgrounds
- Bible History
- Commentary

Author (*Who* wrote the book?)

(1) From the book itself, note all internal evidence of authorship.

(2) Name others to whom authorship is attributed and give arguments for each.

(3) List the main arguments (internal and external) for the traditional authorship.

Date (*When* was the book written?)

(1) What internal evidence sheds light on the time of writing?

(2) List the dates suggested by the different theories.

(3) Are the date and origin in any way determined by the destination? Explain.

BACKGROUND OF PHILIPPIANS

Origin (*From where* was the book written?)

(1) What internal evidence indicates the place of writing?

(2) List the places suggested for the origin of the book and state briefly the arguments for each.

Destination (*To whom* was the book written?)

(1) Note internal evidence of the destination.

(2) List the theories and summarize the issues regarding the destination.

(3) Locate the maps and information covering Paul's missionary journeys in a Bible atlas. Read the written commentary about Paul's journeys in the atlas. Find the place of origin and the place of destination of Philippians on the map(s). Trace Paul's journeys on the map(s). Note the two journeys in which he visited Philippi. Sketch here a simple map of the Roman world and indicate where Rome and Philippi are located.

Occasion (*Why* was the book written?)

(1) What is revealed in the book to be the purpose of the writing?

(2) Explain the background leading to the writing of the book.

Peculiarities (List any *distinguishing features* about the book.)

Biographical Background

A biographical study of the main human personality involved in the book (usually the author, but not necessarily) is a great help in the study of a Bible book. Other characters may be listed and studied also.

The Bible is about human beings! It contains vast biographical material. You should give a great deal of attention to the people of the Bible. Don't lose sight of the "personal touch" in Bible study.

Proceed as follows into a main study of the personalities connected with the Book of Philippians.

Main Character (In this case, Paul)

(1) Who is the main human personality involved in the book? (This person is usually the author, but the book may be about another principal character besides the author.) Write this person's name at the top of the page entitled "Biblical Biography Outline" (see next major heading).

(2) Confine the biblical investigation of each character to the particular book being studied in an effort to see the relationship of his life to the message of the text. As you scan the book, record significant facts about this person on the page entitled "Biblical Biography Outline."

(3) Consult a Bible dictionary and/or a biblical character study. Add helpful notes to your outline after reading the article about this person.

Note: A more extensive biographical study may be made on any Bible personality in the following manner:

a. By using an analytical concordance, find every passage referring to the character and record the significant contribution of each.

b. Then organize the material according to the suggested biblical biography outline. Each point in the parentheses could be a subheading. Other headings could be added.

c. Consult biblical character studies and similar writings about the person and expand your own outline with helpful notes gleaned from these references.

Biblical Biography Outline
Character: _____

1. Background (parentage, place and circumstances of birth, early training and experience)

2. Conversion and Call (conversion experience, call to a specific task, early experience in the ministry)

3. Ministry (its nature, others' reaction to it)

4. Chronology (chronological outline of his life)

5. Character evaluation (good and bad points, including relationships with other people)

6. His death and thoughts about it

7. Lessons learned from this life (and why included in the Bible narrative)

Other Characters

(1) Now list the other important names mentioned in the book along with the verse references dealing with them.

(2) Taking each of these names one at a time, first note significant facts about the person revealed in the book itself. You need not outline these facts as you did for the main character but simply list the facts one after another as you observe them.

(3) Then read the article about the person in a Bible dictionary and add helpful notes about the person.

   (a) Timothy (Phil. 1:1; 2:19,24)

   (b) Epaphroditus (Phil. 2:25-30)

   (c) Euodia and Syntyche (Phil. 4:2)

(d) Clement (Phil. 4:3)

Historical-Geographical Background

Helpful facts should be noted about the historical setting of the book and the main geographical area dealt with in the book. See where the book fits historically in the lives of the writer, recipients of the book, and in God's plan for Israel or the church. Also consider geographical factors—the place (its land, cities, bodies of water) and people (how they lived and thought, their customs, and the conditions of their time).

Consult Related Scripture

Using your general knowledge and a concordance and/or cross-references in your Bible, make helpful notes from other passages of Scripture outside the Book of Philippians that shed light on the historical and geographical setting of the book. (For example, Paul's experiences in Ephesus and the surrounding area as recorded in Acts would be investigated in a study of the Book of Ephesians. In a study of Daniel and his captivity, consult 2 Chron. 36; 2 Kings 24.)

Consult Bible Study Tools

From reading at least one of these tools—Bible encyclopedia, atlas, history, or geography—record helpful facts about the historical setting of the book, main geographical area dealt with in the book, and to whom the book was written. (Look under the book's title, geographical names, and related sections under "chronology.")

7
Overall View of Philippians

You have viewed the *frame* of Philippians in your study of its background. Now you are ready to move into phase two, which is the picture itself, an *overall view* of its basic content as illustrated here.

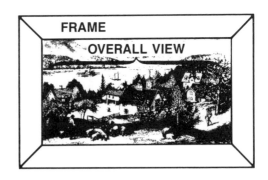

To get the overall view of Philippians, you will be making a *synthetical* study. *Synthesis* means "putting together." In a synthetical study all the parts are "put together" so that the overall picture of the book may be seen. The following six items are covered in the synthetical study. Find what answers you can from looking at the book itself. Then consult one or two tools for additional answers.

Tools for overall view:

- Study Bible
- Bible Dictionary, Encyclopedia
- Bible Handbook
- Bible Survey
- Commentary

Synthetical Study

Theme

(1) Scan the Book of Philippians to determine what idea is uppermost in the mind of the author. State the main theme that is presented in the book.

(2) Consult one or two "tools" and make additional notes regarding the theme of Philippians.

Key Verse

List the one verse or short passage that you think best states the theme of the book.

Key Words

What key words and phrases occur a number of times in Philippians?

Development

To see the development of a book is to see the unity of thought as it progressively unfolds in the course of the writing. After scanning Philippians, list the key ideas that the author presents in his development of the theme. (Note: Do not look for a detailed "outline" of the book at this point. The outline will come later. Simply note the "development" of the basic idea of each chapter relative to the major theme of the book.)

Relation To Other Books

Consult one of the tools that speaks of the relation of Philippians to other books of the Bible. From this source, briefly note here what is said about the relation of Philippians to other books.

Following are some ideas of what is meant by "relation to other books":
(1) Books with which it is grouped (such as "Prison Epistles")
(2) How it is similar to certain other books of the Bible and how its message complements those books
(3) How its message is different (distinctive) from that of other books
(4) Any other "relational" characteristics pointed out in the "Tools"

Tools most likely to show "relation to other books":

- Bible Handbook
- Bible Survey
- Study Bible
- Bible Dictionary or Encyclopedia
- Commentary on the Book

Outline

The following outline follows the New American Standard Version paragraph divisions of Philippians. As you scan Philippians, write a one-line title for each paragraph (indicated by letters and arabic numerals). Then write a one-line title for each major heading (indicated by Roman numerals) that takes into consideration the grouping of related paragraphs underneath the major heading.

Greeting (1:1-2)
  I. (1:3-11):_____
    A. (1:3-8):_____
    B. (1:9-11):_____
 II. (1:12-26):_____
    A. (1:12-18):_____
    B. (1:19-26):_____
III. (1:27—2:18):_____
    A. (1:27—2:4):_____
    B. (2:5-11):_____
    C. (2:12-18):_____
 IV. (2:19-30):_____
    A. (2:19-24):_____
    B. (2:25-30):_____
  V. (3:1—4:1):_____
    A. (3:1-16):_____
      1. (3:1-7):_____
      2. (3:8-16):_____
    B. (3:17—4:1):_____
 VI. (4:2-23):_____
    A. (4:2-9):_____
    B. (4:10-20):_____
Salutation and Benediction (4:21-23)

After composing your own outline of Philippians, compare your outline with the outlines presented by three other writers. From the comparison of their outlines with yours, combine the best ideas to compose a final outline of the book. Another blank outline is provided for your final outline.

Greeting (1:1-2)
  I. (1:3-11):_____
    A. (1:3-8):_____
    B. (1:9-11):_____

  II. (1:12-26):_____

      A. (1:12-18):_____

      B. (1:19-26):_____

 III. (1:27—2:18):_____

      A. (1:27—2:4):_____

      B. (2:5-11):_____

      C. (2:12-18):_____

 IV. (2:19-30):_____

      A. (2:19-24):_____

      B. (2:25-30):_____

  V. (3:1—4:1):_____

      A. (3:1-16):_____

         1. (3:1-7):_____

         2. (3:8-16):_____

      B. (3:17—4:1):_____

 VI. (4:2-23):_____

      A. (4:2-9):_____

      B. (4:10-20):_____

Salutation and Benediction (4:21-23)

PART IV

ANALYTICAL STUDY OF A BOOK

8
Study by Segments and Stages

Since you have come this far in this book, I am sure you desire to learn the practical methods of studying the Bible on your own. I believe you will accomplish this as you work through six simple stages of analytical study in Philippians. Ready, set, here we go!

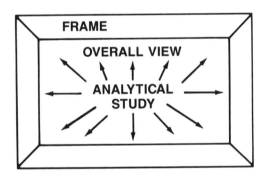

You have covered two phases of a book study—the *frame* and *overall view*. Now you are ready to move into phase three—the *analytical study*, as illustrated here.

Analysis means "breaking up into parts." In Bible study it involves a detailed study of a passage through verses and words, thus a "snail's eye" investigation of it.

In the analytical study, you should take the book one segment at a time and make an extensive, detailed study of it. To divide the book into segments is to provide "bite sizes" for a systematic study of its contents. The best means of dividing the book into segments is to break up the outline (as developed in Lesson 7) into segments of ten to fifteen verses each, breaking each segment at a logical breaking point according to the outline. Let's divide Philippians into eleven segments, as follows:

Segment	1:	Philippians	1:1-11 (11 vv.)
Segment	2:	Philippians	1:12-26 (15 vv.)
Segment	3:	Philippians	1:27—2:4 (15 vv.)
Segment	4:	Philippians	2:5-11 (7 vv.)
Segment	5:	Philippians	2:12-18 (7 vv.)
Segment	6:	Philippians	2:19-30 (12 vv.)
Segment	7:	Philippians	3:1-7 (7 vv.)
Segment	8:	Philippians	3:8-16 (9 vv.)
Segment	9:	Philippians	3:17—4:1 (6 vv.)
Segment	10:	Philippians	4:2-9 (8 vv.)
Segment	11:	Philippians	4:10-23 (14 vv.)

Luther said he studied his Bible in the same way he gathered apples. First, he shook the whole tree so that the ripest fruit might fall. Then he climbed the tree and shook each limb. When he had shaken each limb, he shook each branch, and twig. Then he looked under each leaf. Searching the Bible *as a whole* in a survey study is like shaking the whole tree. Studying *book after book* is comparable to shaking every limb. Giving special attention to individual chapters or *segments* is like shaking every branch. Then you shake each twig by a careful study of the *paragraphs* and *sentences*. But don't stop there; look under every leaf by searching the meaning of the *words*.

Now you are ready to begin an analytical study of the first segment—Philippians 1:1-11. The study of this and each of the other segments will be divided into the following six stages:

• *Text/Translations*. Different translations will be compared to see what meanings can be derived from the English text itself.

• *Diagram, Outline, and Paraphrase*. The text itself is "taken apart and put back together" in diagram form. An outline of the segment may also be developed. A paraphrase of the segment may be composed as well. These exercises help you to determine the central truth of the passage and to see the relationship of its various parts.

• *Observations*. Next you will "spill onto paper" all the good ideas that you can mine from the passage in your own observation of its teachings.

• *Cross-References*. Other Bible passages related to the text will be investigated to see what understanding can be gained by "comparing Scripture with Scripture."

• *Commentaries*. Having discovered all that you can for yourself, you will turn to commentaries to see what further help the thoughts of others can contribute to your understanding of the passage.

• *Topical and Word Studies*. In some of the segments, an extended study may be made of a certain word or doctrine presented in the passage.

9
Text/Translations

A comparison of translations helps you to derive the meaning from the English text itself. Sometimes a different translation may have a more understandable way of presenting the thoughts of the Bible writer, thus giving light that did not appear before to the student. Also, technical points may be clarified by a change in punctuation or a rearrangement of words.

This book provides a page for each segment of Philippians in which the text of the *New American Standard Bible* is printed on the left side with the segment outline, and a blank space on the right for notes from other translations. This page is referred to as a "TON page" because it includes *T*ext, *O*utline, and *N*otes.

How to Make "TON Page" Paste-ups

You may want to make "TON page" paste-ups for the purpose of comparing translations for future studies of Bible books. Cut up two inexpensive copies of the Bible book (or two old Bibles) so that you may have the whole text of the book for the paste-up. Paste the text for each segment of the book on the left side of a sheet of paper. Divide the paste-up under the corresponding headings of the outline of the book that you compose during the synthetical phase of your study of the book (as done in the examples in this book). All the blank space on the right of the paste-up page may be used for making notes of variations in other translations that are compared with that of the text pasted on the left. The diligent student may even want to put paste-ups of three or four translations side-by-side for each segment, thus making his own parallel of translations.

You may prefer to use a parallel of translations, such as *The Four Translation New Testament* (Moody Press) for the same purpose of comparing translations.

The student of the original language may include his own translation of the passage at this point. The remaining phases of the analytical study would include his exegetical (critical analysis and interpretation) study of the passage. An *example* of comparing different translations is seen by the following:

"That ye may approve things that are excellent; that ye may be sincere and without offense till the day of Christ" (Phil. 1:10, KJV).

So that you may be men
of transparent charac-
ter, and may be blame-
less in preparation
for the Day of Christ.
(*Weymouth*)

For I want you always
to see clearly the dif-
ference between right
and wrong, and to be
inwardly clean, no one
being able to criticize
you from now until our
Lord returns.
(*Living Bible*)

So that you may be
unsullied and blame-
less in relation to
anyone's stumbling,
as you face the day
of Christ.
(*Good News Bible*)

Now you are ready for your assignment in comparing translations for segments 1 and 2. *Read* the TON page for Philippians 1:1-11 which follows. Compare the various translations recorded on the page. Notice that key words of special note are italicized. Make notes of your own to capture any ideas that come to your attention as you read the page. After you see how the translations comparison is done for segment 1, you will be ready to do your own for segment 2.

Do the translation comparison for segment 2 (immediately following the page for segment 1). Read the segment in at least three other translations and write in helpful quotes and notes. You may wish to use different translations in the different segments so that you may acquaint yourself with a number of translations.

Tools for translation comparison:
* *New American Standard Bible* (Lockman)
* *New International Version* (Zondervan)
* *The Modern Language Bible* (Zondervan)
* *The Four Translation New Testament* (Moody)
* Paraphrases—*The Living Bible* (Tyndale)
  —*The New Testament in Modern English* (Macmillan)

TON Page (*Text, Outline, Notes*)—Philippians 1:1-11

Greeting (1:1-2)

ᵃPAUL and ᵇTimothy, ᶜbond-servants of ᵈChrist Jesus, to ᵉall the ¹ᶠsaints in Christ Jesus who are in ᵍPhilippi, including the ʰoverseers and ⁱdeacons:
2 ᵃGrace to you and peace from God our Father and the Lord Jesus Christ.

—*slaves* of Jesus Christ (TLB) bondmen (Greek).
—with the *ministers* of the Church and their *assistants* (Weymouth).
—with the overseers and assistants (servants, deacons) (Williams).

1 ¹Or, holy ones
ᵃ2 Cor. 1:1 ᵇActs 16:1 ᶜRom. 1:1; Gal. 1:10 ᵈGal. 3:26 ᵉ2 Cor. 1:1; Col. 1:2 ᶠActs 9:13
ᵍActs 16:12 ʰActs 20:28; 1 Tim. 3:1f.; Titus 1:7 ⁱ1 Tim. 3:8ff.
2 ᵃRom. 1:7

I. Thanksgiving and Prayer (1:3-11)
   A. Thanksgiving for Fellowship (1:3-8)

3 ᵃI thank my God in all my remembrance of you,

4 always offering prayer with joy in ᵃmy every prayer for you all,

5 in view of your ¹ᵃparticipation in the ᵇgospel ᶜfrom the first day until now.

6 *For I am* confident of this very thing, that He who began a good work in you will perfect it until ᵃthe day of Christ Jesus.

7 ¹For ᵃit is only right for me to feel this way about you all, because I ᵇhave you in my heart, since both in my ²ᶜimprisonment and in the ᵈdefense and confirmation of the ᵉgospel, you all are partakers of grace with me.

8 For ᵃGod is my witness, how I long for you all with the ¹affection of ᵇChrist Jesus.

—*Everytime* I think of you I thank my God. Everytime I pray I make my petition for all of you (Berkeley).

—For your *co-operation* (Weymouth/ & Williams).

—will go on to perfect it in preparation for the Day of Jesus Christ (Weymouth).

—will bring it to *completion* (Berkeley).

—for you have a very *special place* in my heart (TLB).

—For God is my witness how I yearn over all of you with tender affection (Weymouth).

—with the *deep felt affection* of Christ Jesus (Berkeley).

—*All* my prayers for you are *full* of praise to God (TLB).

—will keep right on helping you grow in His grace until His task within you is *finally finished* on that day when Jesus Christ returns (TLB).

3 ᵃRom. 1:8
4 ᵃRom. 1:9
5 ¹Or, *sharing in the preaching of the gospel* ᵃActs 2:42; Phil. 4:15 ᵇPhil. 1:7; 2:22; 4:3, 15 ᶜActs 16:12-40; Phil. 2:12; 4:15
6 ᵃ1 Cor. 1:8; Phil. 1:10; 2:16

7 ¹Lit., *Just as it is right* ²Lit., *bonds* ᵃ2 Pet. 1:13 ᵇ2 Cor. 7:3 ᶜActs 21:33; Eph. 6:20; Phil. 1:13f., 17 ᵈPhil. 1:16 ᵉPhil. 1:5, 12, 16, 27; 2:22; 4:3, 15
8 ¹Lit., *inward parts* ᵃRom. 1:9 ᵇGal. 3:26

   B. Prayer For Growth (1:9-11)

9 And this I pray, that ᵃyour love may abound still more and more in ᵇreal knowledge and all discernment,

10 so that you may ¹ᵃapprove the things that are excellent, in order to be sincere and blameless ²until ᵇthe day of Christ;

11 having been filled with the ᵃfruit of righteousness which *comes* through Jesus Christ, to the glory and praise of God.

—And it is my prayer that your love may be more and more accompanied by clear knowledge and keen perception for *testing things that differ,*so that you may be *men of transparent character,* and may be blameless in preparation for the Day of Christ (Weymouth).

—so that you may be unsullied and blameless in relation to anyone's stumbling (Berkeley).

—For I want you always to *see clearly the difference between right and wrong,* and to be inwardly clean, no one being able to criticize you from now until our Lord returns (TLB).

9 ᵃ1 Thess. 3:12 ᵇCol. 1:9
10 ¹Or, *distinguish between the things which*

differ ²Lit., *for* ᵃRom. 2:18 ᵇ1 Cor. 1:8; Phil. 1:6; 2:16
11 ᵃJames 3:18

TON Page (*Text, Outline, Notes*)—
Philippians 1:12-26

II. Paul's Present Circumstances (1:12-26)
   A. Joy in the Gospel's Furtherance in Rome (1:12-18)

12 Now I want you to know, brethren, that my circumstances ᵃhave turned out for the greater progress of the ᵇgospel,

13 so that my ¹ᵃimprisonment in *the cause of* Christ has become well known throughout the whole ²praetorian guard and to ᵇeveryone else,

14 and that most of the [1]brethren, trusting in the Lord because of my [2a]imprisonment, have [b]far more courage to speak the word of God without fear.

15 [a]Some, to be sure, are preaching Christ even from envy and strife, but some also from good will;

16 [1]the latter *do it* out of love, knowing that I am appointed for the defense of the [a]gospel;

17 the former proclaim Christ [a]out of selfish ambition, [1]rather than from pure motives, thinking to cause me distress in my [2b]imprisonment.

18 What then? Only that in every way, whether in pretense or in truth, Christ is proclaimed; and in this I rejoice, yes, and I will rejoice.

12 [a]Luke 21:13
[b]Phil. 1:5, 7, 16, 27; 2:22; 4:3, 15
13 [1]Lit., *bonds*
[2]Or, *governor's palace*
[a]Phil. 1:7; 2 Tim. 2:9 [b]Acts 28:30
14 [1]Or, *brethren in the Lord, trusting because of my bonds* [2]Lit., *bonds*
[a]Phil. 1:7; 2 Tim. 2:9 [b]Acts 4:31;

2 Cor. 3:12; 7:4; Phil. 1:20
15 [a]2 Cor. 11:13
16 [1]Some later mss. reverse the order of vv. 16 and 17
[a]Phil. 1:5, 7, 12, 27; 2:22; 4:3, 15
17 [1]Lit., *not sincerely* [2]Lit., *bonds*
[a]Rom. 2:8; Phil. 2:3 [b]Phil. 1:7; 2 Tim. 2:9

B. Determination to Magnify Christ in Life or Death (1:19-26)

19 For I know that this shall turn out for my [1]deliverance [a]through your [2]prayers and the provision of [b]the Spirit of Jesus Christ,

20 according to my [a]earnest expectation and [b]hope, that I shall not be put to shame in anything, but *that* with [c]all boldness, Christ shall even now, as always, be [d]exalted in my body, [e]whether by life or by death.

21 For to me, [a]to live is Christ, and to die is gain.

22 [1]But if *I am* to live *on* in the flesh, this *will mean* [a]fruitful labor for me; and I do not know [2]which to choose.

23 But I am hard-pressed from both *directions*, having the [a]desire to depart and [b]be with Christ, for *that* is very much better;

24 yet to remain on in the flesh is more necessary for your sake.

25 And [a]convinced of this, I know that I shall remain and continue with you all for your progress and joy in the faith,

26 so that your [a]proud confidence in me may abound in Christ Jesus through my coming to you again.

19 [1]Or, *salvation*
[2]Lit., *supplication*
[a]2 Cor. 1:11 [b]Acts 16:7
20 [a]Rom. 8:19
[b]Rom. 5:5; 1 Pet. 4:16 [c]Acts 4:31; 2 Cor. 3:12; 7:4; Phil. 1:14 [d]1 Cor. 6:20 [e]Rom. 14:8
21 [a]Gal. 2:20
22 [1]Or, *But if to*

live in the flesh, this will be fruitful labor for me, then I [2]Lit., *what I shall choose* [a]Rom. 1:13
23 [a]2 Cor. 5:8; 2 Tim. 4:6 [b]John 12:26
25 [a]Phil. 2:24
26 [a]2 Cor. 5:12; 7:4; Phil. 2:16

10
Reassembly by Diagram

From his early childhood, my son enjoyed taking things apart and putting them back together. I was not surprised when, in his teens, he was able to do this in the overhauling of an automobile engine. One learns through dismantling and reassembling things. Actually, this is true in Bible study also.

The Context of the Passage

An important principle of interpretation of Scripture is to *interpret a passage in the light of its context*. One can prove almost any doctrine by taking certain words of Scripture out of their context and misapplying them to make them mean something other than what the author had in mind. To get the author's true meaning, you must understand where each phrase fits into the overall message of the passage. Each phrase must be seen in its proper relation to the "connected thread" of the whole paragraph, and each paragraph in relation to the entire segment. There are three means for fitting all parts of a passage into the "thread" of its context.

Three Means of Reassembly

You have read the text in different translations to see what meanings can be derived from reading the text. Now you are ready to "take apart and put back together" the passage to determine its central truth and see the relationships of its various parts. Reassembly can be done through one or more of the following means: *diagram*, *outline*, and *paraphrase*. You will be introduced briefly to these three means. Then each one will be covered more fully—the diagram in this chapter, and the outline and paraphrase in the next chapter.

Diagram

A diagram uses only the words of the passage itself in a textual re-creation without the intrusion of comment from outside. By recasting the text in thought pattern, new and wide vistas are opened to the student's eye. Various graphic devices (such as indentations, underlinings, boxing in, colors, and arrows) may be used to show relations within a text. Following is a simple diagram of Philippians 1:1-2:

PAUL and TIMOTHY, bondservants of Christ Jesus,

└─to (1) all **THE SAINTS** (a) in Christ Jesus,
          who are (b) in Philippi,
    (2) including the OVERSEERS and DEACONS:

GRACE to you and PEACE
                from (1) God our Father
                and the (2) Lord Jesus Christ.

Outline

An outline uses different words than those of the text itself to describe the major topics and subtopics of the passage. Philippians 1:1-11 may be outlined as follows:

> Greetings, 1:1-2
> I. THANKSGIVING and PRAYER, 1:3-11
>   A. Thanksgiving for Fellowship, 1:3-8
>   1. When? —always, 1:3-4
>   2. What? —fellowship, 1:5-6
>   3. Why? —concern, 1:7-8
>   B. Prayer for Growth, 1:9-11
>   1. Growth in love, 1:9a
>   2. Growth in discernment, 1:9b-10
>   3. Growth in purity, 1:11

Paraphrase

A paraphrase is a summary of the content of a passage using one's own words to express the ideas presented. The basic thoughts of the passage are written out in paragraph form. Philippians 1:1-3 may be paraphrased as follows:

> From Paul and Timothy, bondslaves of Jesus the Messiah; to all God's consecrated people who live in Philippi, together with their presiding elders and assisting deacons. May God the Father and Jesus Christ His Son give to all of you His blessed favor and heart peace.
>
> Every time I think of you dear Christian friends, I am filled with praise to our Lord for you; and in all my entreaty to God on your behalf, I am filled with delight over you.

All three of the above means of reassembly have in common the aim of "taking apart and putting back together" the text in a different form in order to determine the central truth and the relationships of the ideas of the passage. The difference between the three may be charted as follows:

Diagram	uses the same words of the text	recasts the text in thought pattern
Outline	uses different and fewer words than the text	systematically lists the important parts in major and subheadings
Paraphrase	uses different and probably more words than the text.	rewrites the passage in paragraph form and contemporary language

Diagram

The aim of the diagram is to rearrange the words of a passage in such a way that you can see at a glance the central theme and actual grammatical and thought structure of the passage. The diagram should show the relations of words, clauses, and sentences. The simple kind of diagram suggested here uses only the words of the passage itself in a "textual re-creation" or "mechanical layout" without the intrusion of comment from outside. By recasting the text in a thought pattern, new and wide vistas are opened to the student's eye.

Independent Bible Study, by Irving L. Jensen, is a valuable book on the "inductive method" of Bible study. Its major emphasis is on the construction of a "textual re-creation," similar to the "diagram." Jensen says:

> The purpose of textual re-creation is to pictorialize the Biblical text so that it is made to speak for itself without the intrusion of comment from outside. By so recasting the text in thought pattern, without omitting, adding or altering anything of the text, new and wide vistas are opened to the student's eye in his observations. The re-created text becomes the basic framework about which all other studies are made. . . . Various graphic devices are used to show the many relations within a text. If only one such device were used, the result would be homogeneity in one of two extremes: confusion or fusion. For textual re-creation, therefore, *various* graphic aids should be used such as: indentations, underlinings, large and small capitalizations, small-type letters, circling, boxing, various colors, arrows, and numerical listings, blank spaces, shading. There is no one standard procedure in recreating the text. The best way to learn this step is by doing.[1]

An example of the diagram is given for the first segment of Philippians (1:1-11). A careful investigation of this example diagram will be the best means of reaching an understanding of what is involved in making a diagram of a passage. Then you will want to try to make your own diagram of the second segment (Phil. 1:12-26).

Note the features of the diagram. The diagram should be boxed in. The major divisions of the segment are divided from one another. The word or phrase best capturing the main point of each division is written at the top, right of each division. Key words in the body of the diagram are fully capitalized to cause them to stand out. The verses of each division are noted at the top, left of the division. The diagram takes up about two-thirds of the page (left side). The remainder of the page (right side) is used to note outlines and important observations that are seen while developing the diagram. Various graphic devices (as described by Jensen above) may be used to show relations within a text.

Other names for the textual reassembly that we give the general designation of "diagram" are mechanical layout, textual re-creation, and mechanical reconstruction.

Diagram of Philippians 1:1-11

1-2   **TO THE SAINTS**

PAUL and TIMOTHY, bondservants of Christ Jesus,

     ⌐to (1) all **THE SAINTS** (a) in Christ Jesus,
                    who are (b) in Philippi,
       (2) including the OVERSEERS and DEACONS:

GRACE to you and PEACE
                from (1) God our Father
             and the (2) Lord Jesus Christ.

3-8   **PARTICIPATION**

I THANK my God (1) in all my REMEMBRANCE of you,
            (2) always offering PRAYER
                (a) *with* joy
                (b) *in* my every prayer
                (c) *for* you all,

in view of your **PARTICIPATION** in the gospel
            (1) from the first day
            (2) until now.

For I am CONFIDENT of this very thing,
     (1) that He who began a good work in you
     (2) will perfect it until the day of Christ Jesus.

For IT IS ONLY RIGHT for me to think this of you all,
     (1) because I have you in my heart,
     (2) since both
        (a) in my imprisonment
        (b) and in the defense
        (c) and confirmation of the gospel,
          you are all partakers of grace with me.
     (3) For God is my witness,
        how I long for you all
        with the affection of Christ Jesus.

9-11   **I PRAY**

And this **I PRAY,**

     (1) that your LOVE
        (a) may abound
        (b) yet more and more
        (c) in real knowledge
        (d) and all discernment;
     (2) so that you may APPROVE the things that are excellent,
     (3) in order to be SINCERE and BLAMELESS until the day of Christ;

        having been filled with the fruit of RIGHTEOUSNESS which comes
          (a) *through* Jesus Christ,
          (b) *to* the glory and praise of God.

Extra ideas derived
from the diagram:

The Christian has a
   (a) Position in Christ,
   (b) Place in the world.

Thanksgiving:
   (1) When?

   (2) For what?

      (1) Past
      (2) Present

   (3) Why?

      (3) Future

Support God's servant in his

   (a) Difficulties
   (b) Defenses
   (c) Declarations

Three purpose clauses.

Order for spiritual progress:
   LOVE—DISCERNMENT—PURITY.

"The day of Christ"—

   (1) God's faithful working in His
      disciples (1:6);

   (2) The disciple's perseverance (1:10);

   (3) The discipler's reward (2:16).

Your diagram of Philippians 1:12-26

In the space below make your own diagram of the second segment of Philippians (1:12-26). Your first attempts at the diagram should be sketched roughly on scratch paper. When you think that you have a clear idea of the final form that your diagram should take, make a neat record of it below.

Note

1. Irving L. Jensen, *Independent Bible Study* (Chicago: Moody Press, 1963), 127-128.

11
Reassembly By Outline and Paraphrase

How well did you do on your diagram for Philippians 1:2-26? The diagram is probably the most difficult part of an analytical study. If you did at least 60 percent well, then you won't have any trouble with this chapter and the others to follow. And next time you develop a diagram you'll probably do better! "Practice makes perfect!"

Besides the diagram there are two other ways to dismantle and reassemble a passage in order to see the central teaching and the relationship of the various parts. These two, the outline and the paraphrase, will be covered in this chapter.

Outline

Whereas a diagram uses the words of the passage itself, an outline usually uses different words than those of the text. The outline uses any words that may best summarize the major topics and subtopics of the passage. The key ideas of the passage are delineated in a basic outline form.

Philippians 1:1-11 may be outlined as follows:

> Greetings, 1:1-2
> I. THANKSGIVING and PRAYER, 1:3-11
>   A. Thanksgiving for Fellowship, 1:3-8
>   1. When? —always, 1:3-4
>   2. What? —fellowship, 1:5-6
>   3. Why? —concern, 1:7-8
>   B. Prayer for Growth, 1:9-11
>   1. Growth in love, 1:9a
>   2. Growth in discernment, 1:9b-10
>   3. Growth in purity, 1:11

Now compose an outline for Philippians 1:12-26 (the second segment). The following suggestions will help you.

• Check the original outline of Philippians that you composed during your study of the overall view of the book (see page 47). Use this outline as the basis of your present, more detailed one. All of Philippians 1:12-26 fits well under one heading, which you can make Roman numeral II (to follow Roman numeral I in the above outline of Philippians 1:1-11).

• A study of these fifteen verses will reveal a change in thought at the beginning of verse 19, thus dividing the ideas of verses 12-18 and verses 19-26. Two subheadings may be as follows: A. vv. 12-18, and B. vv. 19-26.

• The framework for these ideas is provided in the following chart. Give titles to the major heading and subheadings. Can you determine whether you should include sub-subheadings and what they should be?

Outline of Philippians 1:12-26:

II. _____, 1:12-26

   A. _____, 1:12-18

   B. _____, 1:19-26

Paraphrase

The paraphrase is a third means of putting together the ideas of a passage in order to get a grasp of its message. Having made a comparison of the translation, a diagram, and an outline of the passage, you now should be able to paraphrase the passage in your own words.

A paraphrase is a summary of the content of a passage that uses one's own words to express the ideas presented. The basic thoughts of the passage are written out in paragraph form. The "Preface" of *The Living Bible* defines a paraphrase as follows:

> To paraphrase is to say something in different words than the author used. It is a restatement of an author's thoughts, using different words than he did. This book is a paraphrase of the Old and New Testaments. Its purpose is to say as exactly as possible what the writers of the Scriptures meant, and to say it simply, expanding where necessary for a clear understanding by the modern reader.
>
> The Bible writers often used idioms and patterns of thought that are hard for us to follow today. Frequently the thought sequence is fast-moving, leaving gaps for the reader to understand and fill in, or the thought jumps ahead or backs up to something said before (as one would do in conversation) without clearly stating the antecedent reference. Sometimes the result for us, with our present-day stress on careful sentence construction and sequential logic, is that we are left far behind.
>
> Then too, the writers often have compressed enormous thoughts into single technical words that are full of meaning, but need expansion and amplification if we are to be sure of understanding what the author meant to include in such words as "justification," "righteousness," "redemption," "baptism for the dead," "elect," and "saints." Such amplification is permitted in a paraphrase but exceeds the responsibilities of a strict translation.[1]

Philippians 1:1-11 may be paraphrased something like the following:

> Timothy and I (Paul), slaves for Jesus Christ, send greetings to the entire congregation of saints who are settled in Christ Jesus and who are situated in Philippi, with warmest regards for the pastors and deacons who labor in your midst.

I am praying that God the Father and our Lord Jesus Christ will bless every one of you with His abundant grace and His abounding peace.

Every time I think about you dear ones I give thanks to God. Every prayer of mine for you is full of joy because of the wonderful way that you have stood with me in the service of Christ ever since the first day you heard His gospel. And I have every assurance that the Lord who started His good work in you will continue to perform His purpose in your life until the glorious day of His return.

I have every reason for feeling so warmly about you as I do. You have a very special place in my heart. You have shown much concern and help for me during the times I was imprisoned and when I was out defending the gospel and proclaiming its good news. God is witness of how deeply I long for you with the tender affection of Christ Jesus.

My prayer for you is that your love for others will continually grow while you increase in spiritual knowledge and discernment, so that you may be persons of transparent character and no one may be able to lay any fault against you from now until Christ returns. May your life always bear an abundance of the fruit of Christ-likeness by His working in you to bring much glory and praise to God.

In accordance with the ideas presented above, write your own paraphrase of the second segment (Phil. 2:12-26). Do not consult a paraphrased copy of the Bible while you make up your own paraphrase of a passage. The exercise will be more meaningful to you if you draw upon your own study thus far (comparison of translations, diagram, and outline) in developing your paraphrase.

Paraphrase of Philippians 1:12-26:

Note

1. From the "Preface" in *The Living Bible,* Paraphrased (Wheaton, Ill.: Tyndale House Publishers, 1971).

12
Observations

What sort of things do you look for when you dig into a study of a Bible passage? This lesson will help you answer that question.

At this point in your analytical study of a passage, you are ready to note your "observations" from the passage. *Observation* is defined as "the art or faculty of taking notice; the act or result of considering or marking attentively." With perceptive eye, you should read the passage, study over your diagram, and look for the types of ideas suggested in the list below.

In making your observations you should record each idea that comes to your attention. If you "spill onto paper" the helpful discoveries that you make of the passage, your mind will be free to dig deeper to find other observations.

John E. Boehmer stresses the "threefold importance of observation":

(1) Because the Bible is verbally inspired, Christians ought to be interested in seeing all that God has inspired—every passage, every verse, every word. No part of God's Word is trivial.

(2) Observation of the Bible is basic to understanding it. Wrong interpretations have often resulted simply because the student did not see or observe all that was in the passage.

(3) Observation adds adventurous delight to Bible study. It makes Bible study a personal discovery, not a spoon-feeding drudgery.[1]

Although this division of study is entitled "Observations," it actually includes and combines three important steps in Bible study—(1) observation, (2) interpretation, and (3) application. Observation answers the question, "What does the passage say?" Interpretation answers, "What does it mean?" Application responds to the question, "What does it mean to me?" These three questions are kept in mind throughout this phase of personal Bible study.

Ideas to Look For

Following is a list of the basic types of ideas that you should look for as you make observations of a passage. Read the list to get an idea of the types of ideas for which you should look. Then when you make your own observations of a passage, come back to the list and follow it closely as a guide in your study until you acquire a working familiarity with the categories of ideas.

Theme

• *Central Truth:* Study the passage to determine its central truth, major emphasis, or theme.
• *Context:* Consider the place of the passage in relation to the outline of the whole book. Consider each idea in relation to the passage as a whole.

• *Key words:* What words keep recurring in the passage? Count the number of times the words appear and give a statement for each as to its meaning and pertinence to the general thought of the passage.

• *Repetitions:* What ideas are repeated throughout a major portion of the passage? Perhaps the same idea is presented in different ways and through the use of various words.

Relationships

• *Similarities:* What relationships are seen between persons, places, events, and ideas?

• *Contrasts:* Having seen items which are alike, now look for those that are unlike or are opposite ideas.

• *Cause and Effect:* What two ideas are grouped together—one as a cause and the other as its effect or one as the source and the other as the channel?

• *Connective Words:* What connective words (such as: after, as, so, before, then, therefore, since, thus, nevertheless, but, likewise, or only) show important relationships?

Other

• *Identification:* Identify persons and places referred to in the passage. Consult tools for more information on these if needed.

• *Definitions:* Note words and phrases that need definitions. Look up the definitions in a concordance or Bible dictionary and explain the words.

• *Figurative language:* Notice pictorial words and ideas in figurative language. What is the key idea conveyed in the imagery used?

• *Problems and questions:* Problems and questions that arise from or are answered by the passage should be noted and studied.

• *Theology:* What is taught in the passage regarding God, Christ, salvation, the last things, or other important doctrines?

• *Principles:* What spiritual principle (fundamental truth or rule) is seen that applies to various situations in life?

• *Application:* Note relevant truths seen in the passage, such as a command to obey, an example to follow, a challenge to take, a warning to heed, a promise to claim, a lesson to remember, an error of living or problem to avoid, or some other application to your personal life.

Observations from Philippians 1:1-11

In the following outline observations are listed for segment 1 (Phil. 1:1-11). The observations are classified under the headings of fifteen types of ideas listed above. Now you will see some examples of the fifteen types of ideas to look for while making observations of a passage.

• *Central Truth:* Paul's relationship to the church is summarized in one word—*fellowship* (participation), his fellowship in winning them, working with them, teaching them, suffering with them, and praying for them.

• *Context:* In vv. 1-11, Paul gave the past, present, and future of the church at Philippi—including a prayer for future growth. This is *introductory* to the whole book. This suggests the following comparison:

> 1:3-11 = past, present, and future of the Philippians;
> 2:5-11 = past, present, and future of Christ; and
> 3:4-14 = past, present, and future of Paul.

• *Key Words*: (1) "I thank" for fellowship and faithfulness of God; and (2) "I pray" for love, discernment, purity. Consider Paul's faithful prayer life!

• *Repetitions:* (1) Three purpose clauses (Greek: *hina, dia, hina*—"that"), vv. 9-11; each leads to the next; three things for which Paul prayed for the Philippians. (2) Three times "the day of Christ" (1:6,10; 2:16). See diagram.

• *Similarities:* (1) "I thank my God in all my remembrance of you," (v. 3) and "And this I pray" (v. 9). (2) "Participation" and "partakers" (vv. 5,7) pictures Christian fellowship. (3) "I thank" (v. 3), "I feel" (v. 7), "I long" (v. 8), and "I pray" (v. 9). (4) Ideas of completion and wholeness: "perfect" (v. 6), "abound" (v. 9), "filled" (v. 11).

• *Contrasts:* (1) Paul referred to himself as a "bond-servant" (slave), and to the Philippian Christians as "saints." (2) Philippians is the only New Testament letter that includes the church officers in the opening greeting.

• *Cause and Effect:* (1) v. 2—God is the source of grace and peace; Christ is the channel. (2) v. 11—"The "fruit of righteousness" comes "through Jesus Christ" (cause or means) and "to the glory and praise of God" (effect or results).

• *Connective Words:* (1) "For" (v. 6)—The basis of confidence in Paul's prayer (vv. 3-5) is seen in verse 6. (2) "For" (v. 7)—The reason for his love and concern for the Philippian Christians is to be given in verses 7 and 8.

• *Identification:* A person: Timothy. A place: Philippi. Both would have been identified in the study under "Philippians Introduction."

• *Definitions:* I should find more information on:overseer, deacons, discernment, and "the day of Christ." Perhaps a more extensive word study should be made on "the day of Christ" when I come to the "topical/word studies" phase.

• *Figurative Language:* (1) "fruit of righteousness" (v. 11)—See "fruit of the Spirit" in Galatians 5:22-23. Moffatt's translation: "life all covered with that harvest of righteousness which Jesus Christ produces." (2) "I have you in my heart"—Greek is: "in the bowels of" indicating the Eastern world view that the seat of emotions was in the stomach area. Today the expression sometimes is used "feel it at gut level." (3) "In all my remembrance of you" may mean not only every time, but every *thing* that he remembered about them was good.

• *Problems and Questions:* What is "the day of Christ"? Judgment, reward, or what? Study this later.

• *Theology:* (1) "The day of Christ is theological. Study it later. (2) Two church officers are listed here and are in the qualification lists of 1 Timothy and Titus—a. pastors, bishops, elders, or overseers; and b. deacons. (3) The perseverance of the saints is recognized by Paul in verse 6.

• *Principles:* (1) Mix praise with petition in prayer: compare "offering prayer with joy" (v. 4) to "with thanksgiving let your requests be made known" (4:6). (2) Note and follow Paul's example of faithful ministry to people. He wrote to them, remembered them, was thankful for them, thanked them and God, intrusted them to God's faithfulness, thought about them, longed for them, and prayed for them.

• *Application:* (1) I should remember in prayer those people to whom I have ministered in past years. (2) I should approve the things that are excellent, seek the gift of true discrimination, and distinguish the things that differ (v. 10). Love for Christ puts one in a better position for spiritual discernment in questionable things.

Do It Yourself

You have read the descriptions of fifteen types of ideas to look for in making observations of a passage. You also have seen examples of these fifteen types from Philippians 1:1-11. Now make a careful study of segment 2 (Phil. 1:12-26) to discover and to record as many observations as you can. The fifteen items will be listed again to guide you, and space will be provided for your notes.

Your Observations from Philippians 1:12-26:

• *Central Truth* (major emphasis, theme)

• *Context* (relationship of an idea to the passage or book as a whole)

• *Key Words* (words that recur)

• *Repetitions* (ideas repeated)

• *Similarities* (relationships between persons, places, events, or ideas)

• *Contrasts* (ideas unlike or opposite)

• *Cause and effect* (or source and channel—how one idea bears on another)

• *Connective words* (after, as, before, but, since, so, then, therefore, etc.)

- *Identification* (of persons or places)

- *Definitions* (words and phrases that need definition)

- *Figurative Language* (imagery, pictorial words)

- *Problems and questions* (that arise from or are answered by the passage)

- *Theology* (God, Christ, Salvation, Last Things, or other important doctrines)

- *Principles* (a fundamental rule that applies to various situations in life)

- *Application* (command, example, challenge, promise, lesson, warning)

Note

1. John E. Boehmer, *How to Study the Bible* (Wheaton, Ill.: Scripture Press Publications, 1965), 15-16.

13
Cross-References

One important principle of Bible interpretation is to "interpret Scripture by Scripture." That is what you should do next in the study of a passage.

Thus far you have studied the English text in several translations, diagramed, outlined, and paraphrased, and have recorded all your own observations from your analytical study of the passage.

Now you are ready to look up other Bible passages that are cross-references to see what understanding can be gained by "comparing Scripture with Scripture." Cross-referencing allows the Bible to be its own interpreter.

By comparing a word or idea with related passages elsewhere in the same Bible book being studied, the author can explain himself. If a discovery is made of the way in which the particular word or idea is treated in *other* books in the Bible, a fuller understanding of the passage is made possible and contradictory interpretations are avoided.

Although there is truth in the statement: "The Bible is its own interpreter," the cross-reference study should not be made until the first three sections outlined above have been completed. Robert Traina gives the reason for this:

> There are some who conceive of the Scriptures as a maze of cross references. As a result, they are constantly searching for similar passages, and they explain each passage in the light of comparable ones. In so doing, they often fail to take the time to examine each unit to discover its singular meaning, and they therefore frequently make erroneous associations. The result is much faulty interpretation.
>
> These statements do not imply that it is invalid per se to use cross references or associate passages. For such a procedure is involved, for example, in an examination of the comparative usage of terms. The danger to which attention is being called is the failure to interpret each unit in its own right before blending various units together. If each passage is first expounded as a literary entity, then valid associations will be made, and such associations will be beneficial. But if there occurs an amalgamation of material before each unit is expounded in view of its own context, then errors in exposition will be the inevitable result.[1]

Use a Bible that has good and sufficient cross-references (such as the NASB) for cross-reference study. Starting with the first cross-reference given for the first verse in the segment being studied, look up every cross-reference given in the complete segment. In some cases you may decide to follow "chain references" that lead you from one related passage to another.

Again, make use of your pen as you "spill your thoughts onto paper." Note any helpful ideas that come to you in this investigation. The suggested list of items under "Observations" in the previous lesson give you ideas of what to look for. Probably not every cross-reference will suggest an observation worth noting.

Cross-References from Philippians 1:1-11

The following is a list of observations made from an exploration of the cross-references for segment 1 (Phil. 1:1-11).

Verse 1

- First verse of 1 and 2 Corinthians, Colossians, Philemon, and Thessalonians: Paul needed to defend his apostleship when writing the Corinthians and Colossians, who questioned it; but not when writing the Philippians, the Thessalonians, and Philemon.
- Acts 16:1: Timothy joined Paul on his second journey, was with him in the establishing of the Philippian church, and was with him in prison.
- Galatians 1:10: Paul was a "servant" who aimed to please Christ, not human beings! (Compare Phil. 1:21).
- Second Corinthians 1:1, Colossians 1:2: The New Testament often calls the church group "saints," but never individuals (seen in checking a concordance). For a possible exception see Philippians 4:21. However, even though "saint" is singular, *panta* (all or every) indicates more than one.
- Acts 20:28; 1 Timothy 3:1f; Titus 1:7: The bishops were overseers to care primarily for the spiritual needs; the deacons were assistants primarily to look after the material needs.

Verse 3

- Romans 1:8: God gives his faithful servants blessed memories that strengthen them when present outward circumstances are difficult.

Verse 5

- "The gospel" in Philippians:
  Fellowship in the gospel (1:5; 4:3,15);
  Furtherance of the gospel (1:12; 2:22);
  Defense of the gospel (1:7,16);
  Faith in the gospel (1:27).

Verse 6

- God's faithfulness until "the day of Christ" (1:6).
  Philippians' faithfulness until "the day of Christ" (1:10).
  Paul's success until "the day of Christ" (2:16).

Verse 7

- A possible translation: "Ye have me in your heart" (ASV). May fit the context better.

Verse 10

- Better translation: "distinguish between the things which differ." This is similar to Romans 1:18. In questionable matters it is difficult for the young Christian to tell the difference between what is right and what is wrong. But when he is truly devoted to Christ, He will give the believer that understanding needed to "distinguish the things that differ."

Your Ideas from Cross-References of Philippians 1:12-26

Make a careful study of cross-references for segment 2 (Phil. 1:12-26), and note any helpful ideas that come to you in this investigation. Again, the suggested list of items under "Observations" in the previous lesson may give you ideas of what to look for in cross-references. Probably not every cross-reference will suggest an idea worth noting. But give diligence to the endeavor to train your mind's eye to find "gems of truth" for yourself. Do your work in the white space provided.

Note
1. Robert A. Traina, *Methodical Bible Study* (New York: Ganis and Harris, 1952), 179-80.

14
Commentaries

Have you been anxious to see what a good commentary has to say about segment 1 or 2 of Philippians? It is best that you restrained yourself from finding out until now. The thoughts of others should wait until you ponder the passage to get all that you can for yourself.

By having made your own personal investigation of the passage to get as much understanding as you could for yourself, now you are ready to see what other people have written about it. You studied the passage itself (text/translations, diagram, outline, paraphrase, and observations). Then you investigated related passages of Scripture to find the Bible's own commentary on itself. Now you are ready to consult commentaries to allow other Bible students to share their insights with you.

Tools for Commentary Study
Commentary on the whole Bible (one volume or multivolume),
Bible studies on individual books,
Sunday School teacher's guides,
Books of expository sermons,
Bible Handbook (limited commentary).

The Value of the Commentary

A commentary is an indispensable help in Bible study, but no commentary is the final word. Compare the ideas received in your original study with those presented in commentaries. In many cases your original ideas will be enhanced by the expressions of others. Where there is a difference, do not be prejudiced to your own interpretations nor misled by another's. Prayerfully open your mind and heart to the illumination of the Holy Spirit, to discover what He actually is saying in the passage.

The Bible commentary, Bible handbook, and similar books give a verse-by-verse or paragraph-by-paragraph explanation of the Bible passage.

John Oakes makes the following comments regarding the value of commentaries:

> Commentaries are an indispensable help to a thorough study of the Bible. They are numerous, of various sizes, and in different numbers of volumes. Some are complete in one volume, some in two, and others in many. They, like other helps, differ in the nature and amount of

material presented. Some are designed for the English-reading student, others for the person with a good working knowledge of the original languages, and others for the person who would study from either angle....

A commentary is not the final word in arriving at the meaning of the Scripture, nor is it intended, as a rule, to be such. Even commentaries differ. They should aid the student in becoming a man of conviction himself as to what the Scriptures say.[1]

Light from Commentaries on Philippians 1:1-11

The following are ideas gleaned from an investigation of four commentaries on Philippians 1:1-11. Read the comments to get an idea of the type of thoughts that are helpful to take notes on when reading in the commentaries. Each idea is numbered for the purpose of distinguishing it. Summaries are not given quotation marks, but direct quotes are:

Ralph P. Martin, *The Epistle of Paul to the Philippians*. Grand Rapids: Wm. B. Eerdmans, 1975.
1. Frequency with which the divine names are mentioned. "The apostle declares unmistakably his Christian faith which is centered in the Persons of the Godhead" (p. 55).
2. Paul doesn't make explicit claim to apostleship in the opening probably because the believers at Philippi did not question his apostleship.
3. "Saints" are separated *from* evil and *to* God.
4. "Their receiving the gospel message and their obedience to it are shown to be genuine by the outworking of the truth in their lives. They had abounded in the grace of unstinting generosity (see 2 Cor. 8:7), and so had proved the sincerity of their love (2 Cor. 8:8) for the Lord and His work" (pp. 60-61).
5. "To think, *phronein*, is a favorite expression of Paul in this letter. Its range and depth of meaning can be seen by referring to 2:2 (twice),5; 3:15 (twice),16,19; 4:2,10 (twice). It means much more than mental exercise, and signifies rather 'sympathetic interest and concern, expressing as it does the action of the heart as well as the intellect' (Michael). It is the outworking of thought as it determines motives, and through motives the conduct of the person involved. A word like 'concern' based on the highest interests of others seems to cover most of the uses of *phronein* in our Epistle" (p. 62).
6. Defense and confirmation are legal terms which describe Paul's trial before the imperial court (compare 2 Tim. 4:16) or his provincial judges.
7. Love—knowledge—judgment. A mental grasp of truth is made possible through God's self-disclosure and received by faith. "A better *knowledge* of God and His ways will promote greater harmony within the fellowship, and give the Philippians a clearer understanding of their mutual relationships as as fellow-believers" (p. 65).

Charles R. Erdman, *The Epistle of Paul to the Philippians*. Philadelphia: The Westminster Press, 1932.
1. Paul "is *advanced in years* or so worn by his labors that he describes himself in a companion epistle as 'Paul the aged.'" "...he *is writing* not to establish doctrines or practice, but to express his gratitude and affection to certain of his friends." In earlier epistles, "he is the acute logician, the profound theologian, the stern defender of the faith. Here he appears as the affectionate friend, the man of tender heart, of human sympathies, of deep emotions, of tears and of joy" (p. 31).
2. Paul included *Timothy* in the salutation. He met Timothy on the first missionary journey. "Paul had a genius for friendship, & Timothy seems to have held the first place in his affection." "The very last of all his letters was written by Paul to Timothy, summoning him to solace his last hour before the aged apostle was led forth to a martyr's death" (p. 33). Timothy, well known to Philippians, was with Paul as he wrote Philippians.

3. "supplication with *joy*" (v. 3)—This word "sounds the keynote of the epistle. Again and again through the passages which follow this glad note will be repeated" (p. 41). (An interesting word study would be to trace "joy" through Philippians.)

A. B. Simpson, *The Epistles to the Philippians and the Colossians.* Harrisburg, Penn.: Christian Publications, Inc. n.d.
1. "While *Ephesians* describes the highest Christian life, *Philippians* portrays the sweetest Christian life" (p. 5)
2. "The first trait that strikes us in this sketch is the affectionateness of Paul's spirit. Sanctification does not take out of our hearts the spirit of tenderness and love. It purifies and intensifies every heart-string. . . . The cords of his sensitive being were alive with tender yearning" (p. 9).
3. *Traits* seen in Paul in chapter 1 are: affection; cheerfulness, hopefulness, and thankfulness; unselfish prayer; fellowship; victory of difficulties and trials; victory over people; devotion to Christ (the secret of all the rest); a holy indifference; and a sublime confidence.
4. *General Gordon*, when the Mahdi threatened him with death, smiled in his face and said, "You could not do me a greater favor than thus quickly to introduce me into the presence of my best Friend, and the enjoyment of my highest reward" (p. 14).
5. "Paul was in a state of mind where the world could neither *attract* nor *distract* him" (p. 15).

Paul S. Rees, *The Adequate Man: Paul in Philippians.* Westwood, N. J.: Revell, 1959.
1. "This salutation includes *sender, subjects,* & *substance*" (p. 17; 1:1-2).
2. In verses 3-8 we see the *joy* of recollection, intercession, participation, and anticipation.
3. "All the *saints*": "Some would say, 'You are a saint if you have been canonized,' which usually means something that occurs long after you are dead. Some would say, 'You are a saint if you have been cleansed,' such cleansing being understood as complete ethical purgation. But the New Testament says, 'You are a saint if you have been claimed'" (p. 19).

Richard R. Melick, Jr., *The New American Commentary*, Nashville: Broadman Press, 1991.
1. "Philippians 1:3-11 forms a unit of thought in two movements. Several factors reveal the unity: the synonyms 'I thank God' (1:3) and 'this is my prayer' (1:9), the general content of praise and petition, and Paul's epistolary pattern in introductions" (p. 53).
2. "The section divides naturally into two subsections, however. First, vv. 3-8 express praise for the Philippians. The verb translated 'I thank my God' contains the idea of thanksgiving. Furthermore, all of vv. 3-8 modify that one main verb. Second, vv. 9-11 express Paul's more specific petition" (p. 53).

Your Notes from Commentaries on Philippians 1:12-26

In the following space, make your own notes from two or more commentaries that you consult on Philippians 1:12-26. Direct quotations should be put in quotation marks. Your own summaries of ideas presented in the commentary need not be put in quotation marks since it will be recognized that every idea on your commentaries page is taken from the specified authors and titles. Number each idea for the purpose of distinguishing it, as was done above.

Note
1. John P. Oakes, *Exploring Your Bible* (Grand Rapids: Zondervan Publishing House, 1960), 102-03.

15
Topical and Word Studies

Now you are ready to get down to "the last word" in an analytical study. In the last phase of the study of a segment, the Bible student looks under the leaf by searching word meanings, as suggested in the illustration from Luther shared earlier in chapter 8.

A topical study and word study are closely related. A topical study deals with a general theme such as "the final rewards for the Christian" and includes the study of related words such as rewards, crowns, the judgment seat of Christ, and promises for faithfulness. Therefore, a topical study may involve the study of a number of related words. On the other hand, a word study deals with a specific word of the original language, such as "reconciliation."

The steps in a topical study and word study are similar:

• *Research.* Look up the word or the topic and its related words in the tools listed below. Make helpful notes from your reading, recording any ideas that are helpful to you in your understanding of the topic.

• *Summary.* Cull from all your notes the key ideas that you learned about the topic. This may be done simply by perusing your notes and marking key ideas with a red pencil.

• *Conclusion.* At the end of your notes, write your main conclusions concerning the topic or word. This may include a clear definition plus an outline of facts about the topic.

Tools for Topical and Word Studies

Bible Dictionary or Encyclopedia—Look up the word or the topic and its related words.

Concordance, cross-references, or a Topical Bible—Look up the key words to find their use in other verses.

Translations—Check the passages under consideration in various translations.

Commentaries—Check a few commentaries on the passages containing the topic or word.

Linguistic tools or word studies—Consult books that present a study of the word in its original language.

Theology books and books on particular Bible subjects

Webster's Dictionary of English words also is helpful in the study of Bible words.

A Topical Study in Philippians 1:1-11

Possible words or topics for special study in Philippians 1:1-11 are:
> bondservants (v. 1)
> overseers (v. 1)
> deacons (v. 1)
> Paul's prayer life (vv. 3-11)
> the day of Christ (vv. 6,10)
> discernment (v. 9)
> sincere (v. 10)
> blameless (v. 10)

A Study of "the Day of Christ"

Since "the day of Christ" appears twice in this segment as well as in 2:16, it is selected for an example of a topical study. After deciding what word(s) and/or topic(s) you wish to study in a segment, do for each one the following three things done for "the day of Christ."

Research

Look up the word or topic and its related words in various tools. Some helpful findings regarding "the day of Christ" are as follows.

(1) Greek

Words: *hemeras* (the day) *Christou Iesou* (of Christ Jesus), (v. 6); *hemeran* (the day) *Christou* (of Christ), (v. 10; 2:16).

Hemeran: a natural day; a civil or legal day; a day appointed for very special purposes, especially of a day of final judgment; or a longer period, as a time characterized by a particular activity or trend (as "day of evil"). Used largely in the New Testament as the day on which the Son of Man reveals Himself; Christ is the Lord of this day. (Luke 17:24; 1 Cor. 1:8; 2 Cor. 1:14; Phil. 1:6,10; 2:16) [W. F. Arndt and F. W. Gingrich, *A Greek-English Lexicon of the New Testament and Other Christian Literature* (Chicago: The University of Chicago Press, 1957), 346-47.]

(2) Concordance

There are numerous occurrences of "day" in the Old and New Testaments. Scanning the New Testament references in *Young's Analytical Concordance* (KJV) brings the following ideas:
> "that great and notable day" (Acts 2:20);
> "the day of wrath and revelation" (Rom. 2:5);
> "The night is far spent, the day is at hand" (Rom. 13:12);
> "be blameless in the day of our Lord Jesus Christ" (1 Cor. 1:8; see 5:5).
> "the day of the Lord so cometh as a thief" (1 Thess. 5:2);
> "which the Lord...shall give me at that day" (2 Tim. 4:8);
> "as ye see the day approaching" (Heb. 10:25);
> "by your good works...glorify God in the day of visitation" (1 Pet. 2:12);
> "hasting unto the coming of the day" (2 Pet. 3:12);
> "that we may have boldness in the day of judgment" (1 John 4:17);
> "battle of that great day of God almighty" (Rev. 16:14).

(3) Bible Dictionary/Encyclopedia

The NT idea is pervaded with the elements of hope and joy and victory. . . . In the NT also, however, there is a dark background to the bright picture, for it still remains a "day of wrath" (Rom. 2:5f.). . . . To the unbeliever, the NT depicts it as a day of terror; to the believer, as a day of joy. For on that day Christ will raise the dead, especially His own dead, the bodies of those that believed in Him. . . . In that day He comes to His own (Mt. 16:27-28), and therefore it is called "the day of our Lord Jesus" (2 Cor. 1:14), "the day of Jesus Christ" or "of Christ" (Phil. 1:6,10), the day when there "shall appear the sign of the Son of man in heaven" (Mt. 24:30). All Pauline literature is especially suffused with this longing for the Parousia, the day of Christ's glorious manifestation. The entire conception of that day centers therefore in Christ and points to the everlasting establishment of the kingdom of heaven, from which sin will be forever eliminated. [Henry E. Dosker, "Day of the Lord," in the *International Standard Bible Encyclopedia,* 4 vols. (Grand Rapids: Wm. B. Eerdmans, 1979-88), 1:879.]

(4) Commentaries

God's redeeming and renewing work will reach its crown and climax at *the day of Jesus Christ.* He who began the work of redemption will continue to perform it until its completion at the final day when the Lord returns. The thought here stresses not only the sovereign initiative of God in salvation (compare the wording of Acts 16:14, describing the first Philippian convert), but also the sovereign faithfulness of God in Christ. It reveals Paul's unshakable confidence that the community at Philippi will be preserved in spite of its sufferings and in the face of assaults which are leveled against it (i. 28, ii. 15, iii. 17 *ff.*). [Ralph P. Martin, *The Epistle of Paul to the Philippians* (Grand Rapids: Wm. B. Eerdmans, 1975), 61-62, on Philippians 1:6.]

The "day of the Lord" and the "day of Christ" in the New Testament refer to the time when Jesus returns in fulfillment of His promise to believers in John 14:3. It is the day when Christ will bring humanity's day of rebellion to an end. It no doubt refers to the same day as the *parousia* of Christ, a period beginning with the descent of the Lord from Heaven into the air (1 Thess. 4:16-17) and ending with His revelation and manifestation to the world (2 Thess. 1:7). [C. F. Hogg and W. E. Vine, *The Epistles to the Thessalonians* (Fincastle, Va.: Scripture Truth Book Company, 1959), 150-53.]

Christ Jesus' Day, the Day of His promised Return, and of our glorification with Him. [H. C. G. Moule, *Philippian Studies: Lessons in Faith and Love from St. Paul's Epistle to the Philippians* (Grand Rapids: Zondervan Publishing House, n.d.), 27.]

. . . until Christ again appears. This "day" of his appearing will be the time when the task is complete. Until then, the "gospel of the kingdom . . . [must] be preached in the whole world for a testimony unto all nations." [Charles R. Erdman, *The Epistle of Paul to the Philippians* (Philadelphia: The Westminster Press, 1932), 42.]

"No doubt the reference to the 'day of Christ Jesus' is the 'day of the Lord' so common in the Old Testament (Joel 2:1; Amos 5:20). The question is why the end times were included at this point. . . . Paul's use of the phrase 'until the day' actually called to mind the consummation of the present age. It was Paul's way of making two emphases: sanctification was an ongoing process and the process would continue to the end of the age. At that time the believers would be complete in character. They needed not to fear the judgment which characterized that day." [Richard R. Melick, Jr., *The New American Commentary* (Nashville: Broadman Press, 1991), 59.]

(5) Theology

> The idea of judgment is paramount in all of the many uses of the idea of *the day, that day,* or *the great day* in the Old Testament.... It is concluded that the Day of the Lord is that extended period of time beginning with God's dealing with Israel after the rapture at the beginning of the tribulation period and extending through the second advent and the millennial age unto the creation of the new heavens and new earth after the millennium. [J. Dwight Pentecost, *Things To Come* (Findlay, Ohio: Dunham Publishing Co., 1958), 230-31.]

Summary

In the second phase of a topical/word study you should cull from all your notes the key ideas that you learned about the topic. This may be done by perusing the above notes on "the day of Christ" and marking key ideas with a red pencil. From the notes and key ideas marked you will be able to draw up a conclusion.

Conclusion

At the end of your study of a topic/word, write out your main conclusions concerning the topic/word. This may include a clear definition plus an outline of facts about the topic. Following is a sample "conclusion" that may be drawn from the above study of "the day of Christ."

Definition: The "day of Christ" is the period of time at the end of the age when the Son of Man will reveal Himself to all mankind, will climax His redemptive program, and will defeat all His enemies. He is Lord of that day—His crowning day.

Importance: The "great and notable day" (Acts 2:20); "that great day of God almighty" (Rev. 16:14); the culmination of the great messianic task.

Includes: Christ's coming to His saints, the rapture and the resurrection of believers, His final dealings with Israel, His judgment of the nations, His millennial reign, the ushering in of the eternal kingdom of heaven.

Will be: (1) for the saved—the day we meet our Savior, a day of reward, victory, glorification; therefore—be faithful, have boldness, be blameless at His appearing; (2) for the unsaved—a day of wrath, the ending of human rebellion.

Its nearness: "The day is at hand" (Rom. 13:12); "will come as a thief" (1 Thess. 3:10).

Your Own Topical or Word Study

Follow the above example and outline in making a topical or word study in segment 2 (Phil. 1:12-26). Select a topic or word from segment 2. Some possibilities are as follows: envy (v. 15), strife (v. 15), defense (v. 16), rejoice (v. 18), salvation or deliverance (v. 19), and hope (v. 20). Read the passage. You may find another word or topic that you prefer to study. Study the topic, following the above example. On your own note paper, take notes following the above outline—Research, Summary, and Conclusion.

16
Continuing Your Study of Philippians

In chapters 8—15, you were given the instructions and examples for making an analytical study of a Bible book. An example was presented for each of the following stages in studying segment 1 (Phil. 1:1-11):

(1) Text/translations
(2) Diagram, outline, paraphrase
(3) Observations
(4) Cross-references
(5) Commentaries
(6) Topical/Word studies

After each example, you applied the instructions in your own study of segment 2 (Phil. 1:12-27).

Now you are ready to study the remaining nine segments of Philippians. With each segment, review the instructions and example from chapters 8—15 until you have a firm grasp on the procedure of an analytical study.

To help you get started in each segment, a TON page (*Text*, *Outline*, and *Note* space) is included in the following pages. Also included under segment 4 are "starter" notes on a topical study of the self-emptying of Christ (Phil. 2:7).

If you cannot cover all six stages outlined above when studying a segment, do at least the two stages that are suggested in each case. The stages that are suggested for each segment have been selected to help you get the most benefit from your study and give you ample experience in each of the six stages involved in an analytical study.

Upon the completion of your study, you will have covered all eleven segments of Philippians (including the dividing of the three reassembly methods—diagram, outline, and paraphrase:

Segment 1: Philippians 1:1-11 (11 vv.)—Example
Segment 2: Philippians 1:12-26 (15 vv.)—All Six steps done by you
Segment 3: Philippians 1:27—2:4 (8 vv.)—Text/Translations
Segment 4: Philippians 2:5-11 (7 vv.)—Topical/Word study ("emptied")
Segment 5: Philippians 2:12-18 (7 vv.)—Diagram
Segment 6: Philippians 2:19-30 (12 vv.)—Outline
Segment 7: Philippians 3:1-7 (7 vv.)—Paraphrase
Segment 8: Philippians 3:8-16 (9 vv.)—Observations
Segment 9: Philippians 3:17—4:1 (6 vv.)—Cross-references
Segment 10: Philippians 4:2-9 (8 vv.)—Topical/Word study ("book of life")
Segment 11: Philippians 4:10-23 (14 vv.)—Commentary

Use your own note paper as needed for the remainder of your study in Philippians.

Bible Book Study Guide

Note that Appendix A, "Bible Book Study Guide," is a concise summary outline of all the methods and stages involved in a comprehensive study of a Bible book as presented in this book. You may wish to make copies of this ready reference sheet to guide you in your future ventures in Bible study.

Segment 3 (Phil. 1:27—2:4)

Assignment: Compare Text/Translations

In an analytical study of a segment, you would want to follow the six steps listed. For now, complete only the first step (capitalized), to gain more experience in comparing translations.

1. TEXT/TRANSLATIONS
2. Diagram/Outline/Paraphrase
3. Observations
4. Cross-references
5. Commentaries
6. Topical/Word studies

Review chapter 9 before doing this assignment. Then do the translation comparison for segment 3. Read the segment in at least three other translations and write helpful notes in the space provided. Acquaint yourself with translations not used before.

III. Exhortations To Live Worthy of the Gospel (1:27—2:18)

    A. Unity (1:27—2:4)

27 Only conduct yourselves in a manner ªworthy of the ᵇgospel of Christ; so that whether I come and see you or remain absent, I may hear of you that you are ᶜstanding firm in ᵈone spirit, with one ¹mind ᵉstriving together for the faith of the gospel;

28 in no way alarmed by *your* opponents—which is a ªsign of destruction for them, but of salvation for you, and that *too*, from God.

29 For to you ªit has been granted for Christ's sake, not only to believe in Him, but also to ᵇsuffer for His sake,

30 experiencing the same ªconflict which ᵇyou saw in me, and now hear *to be* in me.

CHAPTER 2

Be Like Christ

IF therefore there is any encouragement in Christ, if there is any consolation of love, if there is any ªfellowship of the Spirit, if any ¹ᵇaffection and compassion,

2 ªmake my joy complete ¹by ᵇbeing of the same mind, maintaining the same love, united in spirit, intent on one purpose.

3 Do nothing from ¹ªselfishness or ᵇempty conceit, but with humility of mind let ᶜeach of you regard one another as more important than himself;

4 ªdo not *merely* look out for your own personal interests, but also for the interests of others.

27 ¹Lit., *soul* ªEph. 4:1 ᵇPhil. 1:5 ᶜl Cor. 16:13; Phil. 4:1 ᵈActs 4:32 ᵉJude 3
28 ª2 Thess. 1:5
29 ªMatt. 5:11, 12 ᵇActs 14:22
30 ªCol. 1:29; 2:1; 1 Thess. 2:2; 1 Tim. 6:12; 2 Tim. 4:7; Heb. 10:32; 12:1 ᵇActs 16:19-40; Phil. 1:13

1 ¹Lit., *inward parts* ª2 Cor. 13:14 ᵇCol. 3:12
2 ¹Lit., *that you be* ªJohn 3:29 ᵇRom. 12:16; Phil. 4:2
3 ¹Or, *contentiousness* ªRom. 2:8; Phil. 1:17 ᵇGal. 5:26 ᶜRom. 12:10; Eph. 5:21
4 ªRom. 15:1f.

Segment 4 (Phil 2:5-11)

Assignment: Topical/Word Study (The "self-emptying of Christ")

Remember that there are six steps that you would want to follow in an analytical study. For segment 4, concentrate on step number 6, topical/word studies (capitalized in the outline of steps).

1. Text/translations
2. Diagram/Outline/Paraphrase
3. Observations
4. Cross-references
5. Commentaries
6. TOPICAL/WORD STUDIES

Before doing this assignment, review chapter 15. Then make a topical/word study of the self-emptying of Christ taught in Philippians 2:6-8.

B. Humility (2:5-11)

5 ªHave this attitude ¹in yourselves which was also in ᵇChrist Jesus,
6 who, although He ªexisted in the ᵇform of God ᶜdid not regard equality with God a thing to be grasped,
7 but ¹ªemptied Himself, taking the form of a ᵇbond-servant, *and* ᶜbeing made in the likeness of men.
8 And being found in appearance as a man, ªHe humbled Himself by becoming ᵇobedient to the point of death, even ᶜdeath ¹on a cross.
9 ªTherefore also God ᵇhighly exalted Him, and bestowed on Him ᶜthe name which is above every name,
10 that at the name of Jesus ªEVERY KNEE SHOULD BOW, of ᵇthose who are in heaven, and on earth, and under the earth,
11 and that every tongue should confess that Jesus Christ is ªLord, to the glory of God the Father.

5 ¹Or, *among* ªMatt. 11:29; Rom. 15:3 ᵇPhil. 1:1
6 ªJohn 1:1 ᵇ2 Cor. 4:4 ᶜJohn 5:18; 10:33; 14:28
7 ¹I.e., laid aside His privileges ª2 Cor. 8:9 ᶜJohn 1:14; Rom. 8:3; Gal. 4:4; Heb. 2:17
8 ¹Lit., *of* ª2 Cor. 8:9 ᵇMatt. 26:39; John 10:18; Rom. 5:19; Heb. 5:8 ᶜHeb. 12:2
9 ªHeb. 1:9 ᵇMatt. 28:18; Acts 2:33; Heb. 2:9 ᶜEph. 1:21
10 ªIs. 45:23; Rom. 14:11 ᵇEph. 1:10
11 ªJohn 13:13; Rom. 10:9; 14:9

Philippians 2 says that Christ "existed in the form of God...but emptied Himself, taking the form of a bond-servant." The question arising from this is: *Of what did Christ empty Himself?* To find the answer to this question, follow the three steps as outlined below.

Research

(1) First, write observations that you gain from the context. Note what each phrase below teaches you about the self-emptying of Christ:

v. 6: "did not regard equality with God a thing to be grasped"

v. 7: "but emptied Himself"

"taking the form of a bond-servant"

"being made in the likeness of men"

v. 8: "And being found in appearance as a man, He humbled Himself"

"by becoming obedient"

"to the point of death, even death on a cross"

(2) Next, look up cross references on each of these seven phrases, and note here any ideas that bear on the meaning of Christ's self-emptying.

(3) The following are notes taken from various tools consulted on the question of Christ's self-emptying. What conclusions would you draw from these notes? Perhaps you will want to underline key ideas revealed in the notes.

• *Young's Analytical Concordance: kenoo*—make of none effect (1 Cor. 1:17); make of no reputation (Phil. 2:7); make void (Rom. 4:14, 1 Cor. 9:15); be in vain (2 Cor. 9:3). *Kenos*— empty (Mark 12:3; Luke 1:53; 20:10,11); vain (Acts 4:25; 1 Cor. 15:10,14,58; 2 Cor. 6:1; Gal. 2:2; Eph. 5:6; Phil. 2:16; Col. 2:8; 1 Thess. 2:1; 3:5; Jas. 2:20; 4:5).

• Cross-References: "[Jesus] came not to be ministered unto, but to minister, and to give his life a ransom for many."—Matt. 20:28, KJV. "For ye know the grace of our Lord Jesus Christ, that, though he was rich, yet for your sakes he became poor, that ye through his poverty might become rich."—2 Cor. 8:9, KJV.

• Translations: Conybeare and Howson: "stripped himself (of his glory)." *The Amplified New Testament:* "Who, although being essentially one with God and in the form of God [possessing the fullness of the attributes which make God God], did not think this equality with God was a thing to be eagerly grasped or retained" (Phil. 2:6).

• *The New Bible Dictionary:*

> It refers to the "pre-incarnate renunciation coincident with the act of 'taking the form of a servant'" (V. Taylor, *The Person of Christ in New Testament Teaching*, 1958, p. 77). His taking of the servant's form involved the necessary limitation of the glory which he laid aside that he might be born 'in the likeness of men'.... The 'kenosis' then began in his Father's presence with his preincarnate choice to assume our nature; it led inevitably to the final obedience of the cross when he did, to the fullest extent, pour out his soul unto death (see Rom. 8:3; 2 Cor. 8:9; Gal. 4:4-5; Heb. 2:14-16; 10:5ff.)."[1]

• *The Epistle to the Philippians,* F. B. Meyer:

> He voluntarily laid aside the exercise of His omnipotence, that He might receive power from God; absolutely and voluntarily forewent the use of attributes that lay all around Him, like tools within the reach of the skilled mechanic, that He might live a truly human life, weeping our tears, and receiving the plenitude of His Father's power.[2]

• *The New American Commentary*, Richard R. Melick, Jr.:

> The verb 'emptied' (NASB) does not require a knowledge of what was emptied (Rom. 4:14; 1 Cor. 1:17; 9:15). Often it is translated simply 'to render void, of no effect.' This passage affirms simply that Christ left his position, rank, and privilege. They were 'of no effect.' (Note: "The most that can be said is that Jesus left the appearance of deity to accept another form of existence.... It is best to leave unanswered questions the text does not raise and, therefore, does not answer.")[3]

• *Systematic Theology,* Louis Berkhof:

> Now what does His becoming a servant involve? A state of subjection in which one is called upon to render obedience. And the opposite of this is a state of sovereignty in which one has the right to command. The being on an equality with God does not denote a mode of being, but a state which Christ exchanged for another state.[4]

• *The Doctrine of Man,* A. H. Strong:

> In this act, he resigned not the possession, nor yet entirely the use, but rather the independent exercise, of the divine attributes." This humiliation consisted further "In the submission of the Logos to the control of the Holy Spirit and the limitations of his Messianic mission, in his communication of the divine fulness to the human nature which he had taken into union with himself." And finally it consisted "In the continuous surrender, on the part of the God-man, so far as his human nature was concerned, of the exercise of those divine powers with which it was endowed by virtue of its union with the divine, and in the voluntary acceptance, which followed upon this, of temptation, suffering, and death.[5]

(4) Do some additional reading on your own regarding the subject of Christ's "emptying" and add notes here.

Summary

Briefly summarize your findings from all the above research by underlining in red the key ideas.

Conclusion

Write out your main conclusions concerning the meaning of the emptying of Christ in Philippians 2:7.

Segment 5 (Phil. 2:12-18)

Assignment: Diagram

Review chapter 10 before beginning work on this assignment. Remember that the diagram is one of three means of reassembly. The diagram uses only the words of the passage itself in a textual re-creation, and enables you to see at a glance the central theme and the actual grammatical and thought structure of the passage.

1. Text/translations
2. DIAGRAM/Outline/Paraphrase
3. Observations
4. Cross references
5. Commentaries
6. Topical/word studies

Using the example of the diagram of the first segment and your own diagram of the second segment make a diagram of Philippians 2:12-18.

C. Steadfastness

12 So then, my beloved, ªjust as you have always obeyed, not as in my presence only, but now much more in my absence, work out your ᵇsalvation with ᶜfear and trembling;

13 for it is ªGod who is at work in you, both to will and to work ᵇfor *His* good pleasure.

14 Do all things without ªgrumbling or disputing;

15 that you may ¹prove yourselves to be ªblameless and innocent, ᵇchildren of God above reproach in the midst of a ᶜcrooked and perverse generation, among whom you ²ᵈappear as ³lights in the world,

16 holding ¹fast the word of life, so that in ªthe day of Christ I may have cause to glory because I did not ᵇrun in vain nor ᶜtoil in vain.

17 But even if I am being ªpoured out as a drink offering upon ᵇthe sacrifice and service of your faith, I rejoice and share my joy with you all.

18 And you too, *I urge you*, rejoice in the same way and share your joy with me.

12 ªPhil. 1:5, 6; 4:15 ᵇHeb. 5:9 ᶜ2 Cor. 7:15
13 ªRom. 12:3; 1 Cor. 12:6; 15:10; Heb. 13:21 ᵇEph. 1:5
14 ª1 Cor. 10:10; 1 Pet. 4:9
15 ¹Or, *become* ²Or, *shine* ³Or, *luminaries, stars* ªLuke 1:6; Phil.
3:6 ᵇMatt. 5:45; Eph. 5:1 ᶜDeut. 32:5; Acts 2:40 ᵈMatt. 5:14-16
16 ¹Or, *forth* ªPhil. 1:6 ᵇGal. 2:2 ᶜIs. 49:4; Gal. 4:11; 1 Thess. 3:5
17 ª2 Cor. 12:15; 2 Tim. 4:6 ᵇNum. 28:6, 7; Rom. 15:16

Segment 6 (Phil. 2:19-30)

Assignment: Outline Paul's Plans to Send Help

1. Text/translations
2. Diagram/OUTLINE/Paraphrase
3. Observations
4. Cross-references
5. Commentaries
6. Topical/Word studies

Review chapter 11 before doing this assignment. Compose an outline of Philippians 2:19-30. Refer to your overall outline before beginning.

IV. Paul Planned to Send Help to Philippi—Two examples of humility (2:19-30)

    A. To Send Timothy Soon (2:19-24)

Timothy and Epaphroditus

19 But I hope [1]in the Lord Jesus to [a]send [b]Timothy to you shortly, so that I also may be encouraged when I learn of your condition.
20 For I have no one *else* [a]of kindred spirit who will genuinely be concerned for your welfare.
21 For they all [a]seek after their own interests, not those of Christ Jesus.
22 But you know [a]of his proven worth that [b]he served with me in the furtherance of the gospel [c]like a child *serving* his father.
23 [a]Therefore I hope to send him immediately, as soon as I see how things *go* with me;
24 and [a]I trust in the Lord that I myself also shall be coming shortly.

19 [1]Or, *trusting in*
[a]Phil. 2:23 [b]Phil. 1:1
20 [a]1 Cor. 16:10; 2 Tim. 3:10
21 [a]1 Cor. 10:24; 13:5; Phil. 2:4
22 [a]Rom. 5:4; Acts 16:2 [b]Acts 16:3; 1 Cor. 16:10; 2 Tim. 3:10 [c]1 Cor. 4:17
23 [a]Phil. 2:19
24 [a]Phil. 1:25

B. To Send Epaphroditus Immediately (2:25-30)

25 But I thought it necessary to send to you [a]Epaphroditus, my brother and [b]fellow worker and [c]fellow soldier, who is also your [1][d]messenger and [e]minister to my need;
26 because he was longing [1]for you all and was distressed because you had heard that he was sick.
27 For indeed he was sick to the point of death, but God had mercy on him, and not on him only but also on me, lest I should have sorrow upon sorrow.
28 Therefore I have sent him all the more eagerly in order that when you see him again you may rejoice and I may be less concerned *about you.*
29 Therefore [a]receive him in the Lord with all joy, and [b]hold men like him in high regard;
30 because he came close to death [a]for the work of Christ, risking his life to [b]complete [1]what was deficient in your service to me.

25 [1]Lit., *apostle*
[a]Phil. 4:18 [b]Rom. 16:3, 9, 21; Phil. 4:3; Philem. 1, 24 [c]Philem. 2 [d]John 13:16; 2 Cor. 8:23 [e]Phil. 4:18
26 [1]Some ancient mss. read *to see you all*
29 [a]Rom. 16:2 [b]1 Cor. 16:18
30 [1]Lit., *your deficiency of service* [a]Acts 20:24 [b]1 Cor. 16:17; Phil. 4:10

Segment 7 (Phil. 3:1-7)

Assignment: Paraphrase Paul's Warnings Against Judaizers

1. Text/translations
2. Diagram/Outline/PARAPHRASE
3. Observations
4. Cross-references
5. Commentaries
6. Topical/Word studies

A *paraphrase* is one of the three means of reassembly. Review chapter 11 and write your own paraphrase of Philippians 3:1-7. Before you compose your paraphrase, it may be helpful to read one or two commentaries on the passage to grasp the meanings of some of the words and phrases such as "dogs," "true circumcision," "confidence," "flesh," Hebrew of Hebrews," "Pharisee," "blameless," and "loss."

V. Warning Against False Teachers (3:1—4:1)
    A. Against Judaizers (3:1-16)
        1. Paul's Past—Counted Loss (3:1-7)

CHAPTER 3

The Goal of Life

FINALLY, my brethren, ªrejoice in the Lord. To write the same things *again* is no trouble to me, and it is a safeguard for you.

2 Beware of the ªdogs, beware of the ᵇevil workers, beware of the ¹false circumcision;

3 for ªwe are the *true* ¹circumcision, who ᵇworship in the Spirit of God and ᶜglory in ᵈChrist Jesus and put no confidence in the flesh,

4 although ªI myself might have confidence even in the flesh. If anyone else has a mind to put confidence in the flesh, I far more:

5 ªcircumcised the eighth day, of the ᵇnation of Israel, of the ᶜtribe of Benjamin, a ᵇHebrew of Hebrews; as to the Law, ᵈa Pharisee;

6 as to zeal, ªa persecutor of the church; as to the ᵇrighteousness which is in the Law, found ᶜblameless.

7 But ªwhatever things were gain to me, those things I have counted as loss for the sake of Christ.

1 ªPhil. 2:18; 4:4
2 ¹Lit., *mutilation*; Gr., katatome
ªPs. 22:16, 20; Gal. 5:15; Rev. 22:15 ᵇ2 Cor. 11:13
3 ¹Gr., peritomé
ªRom. 2:29; 9:6; Gal. 6:15 ᵇGal. 5:25 ᶜRom. 15:17; Gal. 6:14 ᵈRom. 8:39; Phil. 1:1;
3:12
4 ª2 Cor. 5:16; 11:18
5 ªLuke 1:59
ᵇRom. 11:1; 2 Cor. 11:22 ᶜRom. 11:1 ᵈActs 22:3; 23:6; 26:5
6 ªActs 8:3; 22:4, 5; 26:9-11 ᵇPhil. 3:9 ᶜPhil. 2:15
7 ªLuke 14:33

Segment 8 (Phil. 3:8-16)

Assignment: Note Your Observations

1. Text/translations	3. OBSERVATIONS	5. Commentaries
2. Diagram/Outline/Paraphrase	4. Cross-references	6. Topical/Word studies

Remember that in an analytical study of a segment, you would follow the six listed steps. For this assignment, however, complete only the third step to gain more experience in the area of *observations*. Review chapter 12. Then note your observations on Philippians 3:8-16.

2. Paul's Present—To Gain Christ (3:8-16)

8 More than that, I count all things to be loss in view of the surpassing value of [1a]knowing [b]Christ Jesus my Lord, for whom I have suffered the loss of all things, and count them but rubbish in order that I may gain Christ,

9 and may be found in Him, not having [a]a righteousness of my own derived from *the* Law, but that which is through faith in Christ, [b]the righteousness which *comes* from God on the basis of faith,

10 that I may [a]know Him, and [b]the power of His resurrection and [1c]the fellowship of His sufferings, being [d]conformed to His death;

11 [1]in order that I may [a]attain to the resurrection from the dead.

12 Not that I have already [a]obtained *it*, or have already [b]become perfect, but I press on [1]in order that I may [c]lay hold of that [2]for which also I [d]was laid hold of by [e]Christ Jesus.

13 Brethren, I do not regard myself as having laid hold of *it* yet; but one thing *I do*: [a]forgetting what *lies* behind and reaching forward to what *lies* ahead,

14 I [a]press on toward the goal for the prize of the [b]upward call of God in [c]Christ Jesus.

15 Let us therefore, as many as are [1a]perfect, have this attitude; and if in anything you have a [b]different attitude, [c]God will reveal that also to you;

16 however, let us keep [1a]living by that same *standard* to which we have attained.

8 [1]Lit., *the knowledge of*
[a]Jer. 9:23f.; John 17:3; Eph. 4:13; Phil. 3:10; 2 Pet. 1:3 [b]Rom. 8:39; Phil. 1:1; 3:12
9 [a]Rom. 10:5; Phil. 3:6 [b]Rom. 9:30; 1 Cor. 1:30
10 [1]Or, *participation in* [a]Jer. 9:23f.; John 17:3; Eph. 4:13; Phil. 3:8; 2 Pet. 1:13 [b]Rom. 6:5 [c]Rom. 8:17 [d]Rom. 6:5; 8:36; Gal. 6:17
11 [1]Lit., *if somehow* [a]Acts 26:7; 1 Cor. 15:23; Rev. 20:5f.
12 [1]Lit., *if I may* even [2]Or, *because also*
[a]1 Cor. 9:24f.; 1 Tim. 6:12, 19 [b]1 Cor. 13:10 [c]1 Tim. 6:12, 19 [d]Acts 9:5f. [e]Rom. 8:39; Phil. 1:1; 3:3
13 [a]Luke 9:62
14 [a]1 Cor. 9:24; Heb. 6:1 [b]Rom. 8:28; 11:29; 2 Tim 1:9 [c]Phil. 3:3
15 [1]Or, *mature* [a]Matt. 5:48; 1 Cor. 2:6 [b]Gal. 5:10 [c]John 6:45; Eph. 1:17; 1 Thess. 4:9
16 [1]Lit., *following in line* [a]Gal. 6:16

Segment 9 (Phil. 3:17—4:1)

Assignment: Look Up Cross-References

1. Text/translations
2. Diagram/Outline/Paraphrase
3. Observations
4. CROSS-REFERENCES
5. Commentaries
6. Topical/Word studies

Review chapter 13 before doing this assignment. Look up other Bible passages that are cross-references to Philippians 3:17—4:1 to see what understanding can be gained by "comparing Scripture with Scripture." Use a study Bible or a tool like *The Treasury of Scripture Knowledge* that provides an extensive list of cross-references. Note any helpful ideas that come to you in this investigation.

B. Against Antinomianism (3:17—4:1)

17 Brethren, ᵃjoin in following my example, and observe those who walk according to the ᵇpattern you have in us.

18 For ᵃmany walk, of whom I often told you, and now tell you even ᵇweeping, *that they are* enemies of ᶜthe cross of Christ,

19 whose end is destruction, whose god is *their* ¹ᵃappetite, and *whose* ᵇglory is in their shame, who ᶜset their minds on earthly things.

20 For ᵃour ¹citizenship is in heaven, from which also we eagerly ᵇwait for a Savior, the Lord Jesus Christ;

21 who will ᵃtransform ¹the body of our humble state into ᵇconformity with ²the ᶜbody of His glory, ᵈby the exertion of the power that He has even to ᵉsubject all things to Himself.

CHAPTER 4

Think of Excellence

THEREFORE, my beloved brethren ¹whom I ᵃlong *to see*, my joy and crown, so ᵇstand firm in the Lord, my beloved.

17 ᵃ1 Cor. 4:16;
11:1; Phil. 4:9
ᵇ1 Pet. 5:3
18 ᵃ2 Cor. 11:13
ᵇActs 20:31 ᶜGal.
6:14
19 ¹Lit., *belly*
ᵃRom. 16:18; Titus
1:12 ᵇRom. 6:21;
Jude 13 ᶜRom.
8:5f.; Col. 3:2
20 ¹Lit.,
commonwealth
ᵃEph. 2:19; Phil.
1:27; Col.

3:1; Heb. 12:22 ᵇ1
Cor. 1:7
21 ¹Or, *our lowly
body* ²Or, *His
glorious body*
ᵃ1 Cor. 15:43-53
ᵇRom. 8:29; Col.
3:4 ᶜ1 Cor. 15:43,
49
ᵈEph. 1:19 ᵉ1 Cor.
15:28
1 ¹Lit., *and
longed for* ᵃPhil.
1:8 ᵇ1 Cor. 16:13;
Phil. 1:27

Segment 10 (Phil. 4:2-9)

Assignment: Topical/Word Study on "the Book of Life"

For good measure, let's do another word study on the subject of "the Book of Life" (Phil. 4:3). First, note the examples given in chapter 15 and in segment 4 in this chapter. Diligently pursue the steps involved in a topical/word study: a. Research (observations, cross-references, and notes from various tools), b. Summary, and c. Conclusion.

1. Text/translations
2. Diagram/Outline/Paraphrase
3. Observations
4. Cross-references
5. Commentaries
6. TOPICAL/WORD STUDIES

VI. Exhortation and Appreciation (4:2-23)
  A. Further Short Exhortations (4:2-9)

2 I urge Euodia and I urge Syntyche to [1][a]live in harmony in the Lord.

3 Indeed, true comrade, I ask you also to help these women who have shared my struggle in *the cause of* the gospel, together with Clement also, and the rest of my [a]fellow workers, whose [b]names are in the book of life.

4 [a]Rejoice in the Lord always; again I will say, rejoice!

5 Let your forbearing *spirit* be known to all men. [a]The Lord is [1]near.

6 [a]Be anxious for nothing, but in everything by [b]prayer and supplication with thanksgiving let your requests be made known to God.

7 And [a]the peace of God, which surpasses all [1]comprehension, shall [b]guard your hearts and your [c]minds in [d]Christ Jesus.

8 Finally, brethren, [a]whatever is true, whatever is honorable, whatever is right, whatever is pure, whatever is [1]lovely, whatever is [2]of good repute, if there is any excellence and if anything worthy of praise, [3]let your mind dwell on these things.

9 The things you have learned and received and heard and seen [a]in me, practice these things; and [b]the God of peace shall be with you.

2 [1]Or, *be of the same mind* [a]Phil. 2:2
3 [a]Phil. 2:25 [b]Luke 10:20
4 [a]Phil. 3:1
5 [1]Or, *at hand*. [a]1 Cor. 16:22 mg.; Heb. 10:37; James 5:8f.
6 [a]Matt. 6:25 [b]Eph. 6:18; 1 Tim. 2:1; 5:5
7 [1]Lit., *mind*

[a]Is. 26:3; John 14:27; Phil. 4:9; Col. 3:15 [b]1 Pet. 1:5 [c]2 Cor. 10:5 [d]Phil. 1:1; 4:19, 21
8 [1]Or, *lovable and gracious* [2]Or, *attractive* [3]Lit., *ponder these things* [a]Rom. 14:18; 1 Pet. 2:12
9 [a]Phil. 3:17 [b]Rom. 15:33

Segment 11 (Phil. 4:10-23)

Assignment: Glean Ideas from the Commentaries on This Passage

Review chapter 14. Then use at least four commentaries to find ideas on Philippians 4:10-23.

1. Text/translations	3. Observations	5. COMMENTARIES
2. Diagram/Outline/Paraphrase	4. Cross references	6. Topical/Word studies

B. Thanks for Their Gift (4:10-20)

God's Provisions

10 But I rejoiced in the Lord greatly, that now at last ᵃyou have revived your concern for me; indeed, you were concerned *before*, but you lacked opportunity.

11 Not that I speak ¹from want; for I have learned to be ²ᵃcontent in whatever circumstances I am.

12 I know how to get along with humble means, and I also know how to live in prosperity; in any and every circumstance I have learned the secret of being filled and going ᵃhungry, both of having abundance and ᵇsuffering need.

13 I can do all things ¹through Him who ᵃstrengthens me.

14 Nevertheless, you have done well to ᵃshare *with me* in my affliction.

15 And you yourselves also know, Philippians, that at the ¹ᵃfirst preaching of the gospel, after I departed from ᵇMacedonia, no church ᶜshared with me in the matter of giving and receiving but you alone;

16 for even in ᵃThessalonica you sent *a gift* more than once for my needs.

17 ᵃNot that I seek the gift itself, but I seek for the ¹profit which increases to your account.

18 But I have received everything in full, and have an abundance; I am ¹amply supplied, having received from ᵃEpaphroditus ²what you have sent, ³ᵇa fragrant aroma, an acceptable sacrifice, well-pleasing to God.

19 And ᵃmy God shall supply ¹all your needs according to His ᵇriches in glory in Christ Jesus.

20 Now to ᵃour God and Father ᵇ*be* the glory ¹forever and ever. Amen.

10 ᵃ2 Cor. 11:9; Phil. 2:30
11 ¹Lit., *according to* ²Or, *self-sufficient* ᵃ2 Cor. 9:8; 1 Tim. 6:6, 8; Heb. 13:5
12 ᵃ1 Cor. 4:11 ᵇ2 Cor. 11:9
13 ¹Lit., *in* ᵃ2 Cor. 12:9; Eph. 3:16; Col. 1:11
14 ᵃHeb. 10:33; Rev. 1:9
15 ¹Lit., *beginning of* ᵃPhil. 1:5 ᵇRom. 15:26 ᶜ2 Cor. 11:9
16 ᵃActs 17:1; 1 Thess. 2:9
17 ¹Lit., *fruit* ᵃ1 Cor. 9:11f.; 2 Cor. 9:5
18 ¹Lit., *made full* ²Lit., *the things from you* ³Lit., *an odor of fragrance* ᵃPhil. 2:25 ᵇEx. 29:18; 2 Cor. 2:14; Eph. 5:2
19 ¹Or, *every need of yours* ᵃ2 Cor. 9:8 ᵇRom. 2:4
20 ¹Lit., *to the ages of the ages* ᵃGal. 1:4 ᵇRom. 11:36

92

LEARNING TO STUDY THE BIBLE

Salutation and Benediction (4:21-23)

21 Greet every [1]saint in Christ Jesus. [a]The brethren who are with me greet you.
22 [a]All the [1b]saints greet you, especially those of Caesar's household.
23 [a]The grace of the Lord Jesus Christ [b]be with your spirit.

21 [1]Or, *holy one*
[a]Gal. 1:2
22 [1]V. 21. note 1
[a]2 Cor. 13:13 [b]Acts
9:13
23 [a]Rom. 16:20
[b]2 Tim. 4:22

Notes

1. R. P. Martin, "Kenosis," in *New Bible Dictionary*, 2d ed., rev. (Wheaton, Ill.: Tyndale House Publishers, 1982), 652.
2. F. B. Meyer, *The Epistle to the Philippians: A Devotional Commentary* (London: The Religious Tract Society, 1905), 86-87.
3. Richard R. Melick, Jr., *Philippians, Colossians, Philemon*, vol. 32 in *The New American Commentary* (Nashville: Broadman Press, 1991), 103.
4. Louis Berkhof, *Systematic Theology* (Grand Rapids: Wm. B. Eerdmans, 1984), 328.
5. Augustus Hopkins Strong, *The Doctrine of Man*, vol. 2 of *Systematic Theology* (Philadelphia: The Griffith & Rowland Press, 1907), 703.

Appendixes

Appendix A
Bible Book Study Guide

Here is a concise summary outline of all the methods and stages involved in a comprehensive study of a Bible book as presented in this book. You may wish to make copies of these two pages as a ready reference sheet to guide you in your future ventures in Bible study.

I. Introduction   Tools to Use
  A. Background (Critical, Biographical,
        and Historical—Geographical Methods)
      1. Critical 1, 2, 3, 4, 6
          a. Author (who wrote it)
          b. Date (when)
          c. Origin (from where)
          d. Destination (to whom)
          e. Occasion (why)
          f. Peculiarities (distinguishing features)
      2. Biographical 1, 2, 3, 4, 7
          a. Main character
              (1) Background   (4) Chronology   (7) Lessons from
              (2) Conversion & call (5) Death   his/her life
              (3) Ministry   (6) Character evaluation
          b. Other characters (whatever you can learn about them)
      3. Historical—Geographical 1, 2, 3, 4, 6, 8, 9, 10, 11
          a. Characteristics of the place and people to whom or about whom the book is written
          b. Where the book fits—(1) Chronologically in history
                                              (2) Theologically in God's plan of redemption
  B. Overview (Synthetical Method) 1, 2, 3, 4, 6, 12
      1. Theme (idea uppermost in the author's mind)
      2. Key Verse (best summarizes the theme)
      3. Key Words (words used most often, and other words basic to the theme)
      4. Development (basic progressive unfolding of the theme)
      5. Relation to Other Books (similarities & distinctions)
      6. Outline (paragraph titles and groupings under major and subheadings)
  C. Bible Study Tools (See Appendix B for specific titles)
      1. Study Bible   6. Bible Introduction
      2. Bible Dictionary,   7. Biblical Character (and
          Encyclopedia   Background) Studies
      3. Bible Handbook   8. Bible Atlas
      4. Bible Survey   9. Bible History
      5. Principles & Methods of   10. Charts & Chronological
          Bible Study   Outlines

11. Archaeology
12. Commentaries
13. Translations/Paraphrases
14. Word-Study
15. Hebrew & Greek Aids
16. Concordance (English)

17. Cross-References
18. Harmonies
19. Topical Bible
20. Theology
21. Special Topics

II. Analysis
   A. Segments (Divide the book into bite-size
      segments, each segment about 10 to 15 verses).
   B. Stages (Analytical and Topical/Word Study Methods)
      Study each segment in six stages, as follows:
      1. Text/Translations. Compare translations and paraphrases to derive
         understanding of the English text (Make T-O-N pages)..13
      2. Reassembly. Discover central truth and relationships by:
         a. Diagram (textual re-creation)
         b. Outline (topics and sub-topics)
         c. Paraphrase (content rewritten in your own words)
      3. Observations. Mine all the ideas you can by looking for:
         a. Theme
            (1) Central truth (major emphasis, theme)
            (2) Context (relationship of an idea to the passage or the book as a whole)
            (3) Key words (words that recur or bear special importance)
            (4) Repetitions (ideas repeated)
         b. Relationships—
            (1) Similarities (relationships between persons, places, events or ideas)
            (2) Contrasts (ideas unlike or opposite)
            (3) Cause and effect (source and channel—how one idea bears on another)
            (4) Connective words (after, as, before, but, since, so, then, therefore, etc.)
         c. Other
            (1) Identification (of persons or places—get further information on these)
            (2) Definitions (words or phrases that need defining)
            (3) Figurative language (imagery, pictorial words)
            (4) Problems or questions (that arise from or are answered by the passage)
            (5) Theology (God, Christ, Salvation, Last Things, or other important doctrines)
            (6) Principles (a fundamental rule that applies to various situations in life)
            (7) Application (command, example, challenge, promise, lesson, warning)
      4. Cross-References. Compare with other Scriptures 1, 16, 17
      5. Commentaries. Further help from other writers. Compare ideas
         received in your original study with the ideas of commentary writers....................12
      6. Topical/Word Studies. Extended study of certain words
         or themes..2, 12, 14, 15, 16, 17, 19, 20, 21
         a. Research (study the topic or word in helpful tools)
         b. Summary (cull from your notes the key ideas learned)
         c. Conclusions (write out your main conclusions—a clear definition plus an outline of facts)

Appendix B
Bible Study Tools

Looking for the right tool? The following question was posed to me in a letter from a pastor: "I honestly feel a great barrenness of soul concerning a mastery of the Scriptures. Do you have any type of bibliography of Bible exposition as a guide in purchasing books to help in study?"

This bibliography is developed as a guide for Christian laymen as well as vocational Christian servants who search for tools that will be most helpful in the study of the Word of God. I have gathered input from other college and seminary teachers in the developing of this list of basic Bible reference book sources.

The classification topics are for your convenience in locating recommended books by subject matter. The list does not include all the books that are valuable. Neither is the exclusion of a given book evidence that it is not recommended. The basic minimum library does not necessarily include all the titles listed, or even one of the books under each topic. The list is an attempt to identify the books that generally are found to be the most helpful in the given areas. Within each category or sub category the books usually are listed in order of preference and recommendation.

1. Study Bible
   Disciple's Study Bible (Holman)
   The New Open Bible, NASB version (Nelson)
   The New Chain-Reference Bible, NIV, F. C. Thompson (Zondervan)
   The NIV Study Bible (Zondervan)

2. Bible Dictionary, Encyclopedia
   a. Dictionary
      Holman Bible Dictionary (Holman)
      The New Bible Dictionary, ed. J. D. Douglas (Eerdmans)
      The Interpreter's Dictionary of the Bible (Abingdon)
      Unger's Bible Dictionary, Merrill F. Unger (Moody)
      Dictionary of Christ and the Gospels, ed. James Hastings (Scribners)
   b. Encyclopedia
      Zondervan Pictorial Encyclopedia of the Bible, 5 vols. (Zondervan)
      International Standard Bible Encyclopedia, 4 vols. (Eerdmans)

3. Bible Handbook
   Eerdmans' Handbook to the Bible (Eerdmans)
   Halley's Bible Handbook (Zondervan)
   Unger's Bible Handbook (Moody)
   Holman Bible Handbook (Holman)

4. Bible Survey
   a. General (Both Testaments)
      The Unfolding Drama of Redemption, William Graham Scroggie (Zondervan)

Explore the Book, 6 vols., J. Sidlow Baxter (Zondervan)
What the Bible Is All About, Henrietta C. Mears (Regal)
  b. Old Testament
  A Popular Survey of the Old Testament, Norman L. Geisler (Baker)
  The Old Testament Speaks: Old Testament History and Literature, Samuel J. Schultz (Harper and Row)
  The Dawn of World Redemption, Erich Sauer (Eerdmans)
  Old Testament Survey, Paul House (Broadman)
  c. New Testament
  New Testament Survey, Merrill C. Tenney (Eerdmans)
  Survey of the New Testament, R. H. Gundry (Zondervan)
  New Testament Survey, Robert G. Gromacki (Baker)
  The Triumph of the Crucified, Erich Sauer (Eerdmans)

5. Principles and Methods of Bible Study
  a. Principles
  Understanding and Applying the Bible, J. Robertson McQuilkin (Moody)
  Bible Hermeneutics, Milton S. Terry (Zondervan)
  Protestant Biblical Interpretation, Bernard Ramm (Baker)
  Knowing Scripture, R. C. Sproul (Inter-Varsity)
  Hermeneutics, H. Verkler (Baker Book House)
  Interpreting the Bible, A. Berkely Mickelsen (Eerdmans)
  b. Methods
  The Joy of Discovery in Bible Study, Oletta Wald (Augsburg)
  Effective Bible Study, Howard F. Vos (Zondervan)
  How to Study Your Bible, Gordon Talbot (Back to the Bible)
  Independent Bible Study, Irving L. Jensen (Moody)
  Twelve Dynamic Bible Study Methods, Richard Warren (Victor)

6. Bible Introduction
  a. General
  General Introduction to the Bible, Norman L. Geisler and William E. Nix (Moody)
  From Ancient Tablets to Modern Translations, David Ewert (Zondervan)
  The History of the Bible in English, Frederick F. Bruce (Oxford)
  b. Old Testament
  A Survey of Old Testament Introduction, Gleason L. Archer (Moody)
  An Introduction to the Old Testament, Roland K. Harrison (Eerdmans)
  An Introduction to the Old Testament, Edward J. Young (Eerdmans)
  c. New Testament
  New Testament Introduction, Donald Guthrie (Inter-Varsity)
  Introduction to the New Testament, Everett F. Harrison (Eerdmans)
  Introduction to the New Testament, 3 vols., Theodor Zahn (Klock and Klock)

7. Biblical Character (and Background) Studies
  The Life and Times of Jesus the Messiah, Alfred Edersheim (Eerdmans)
  The Life and Epistles of Paul, W. J. Conybeare and J. S. Howson (Eerdmans)
  Harper's Encyclopedia of Bible Life, ed. B. M. Bennett and D. H. Scott (Harper & Row)
  Whyte's Bible Characters, Alexander Whyte (Zondervan)
  Great Personalities of the Bible, William S. LaSor (Fleming H. Revell)
  Paul: Apostle of the Heart Set Free, F. F. Bruce (Eerdmans)
  The Apostles, Donald Guthrie (Zondervan)
  Peter, Stephen, James & John: Studies in Non-Pauline Christianity, F. F. Bruce (Eerdmans)

8. Bible Atlas
  The Moody Atlas of Bible Lands, Barry J. Beitzel (Moody)

Macmillan Bible Atlas, Yohanan Aharoni and Michael Avi-Yonah (Macmillan)
Wycliffe Historical Geography of Bible Lands, Charles F. Pfeiffer and Howard F. Vos (Moody)
Baker's Bible Atlas, Charles P. Pfeiffer (Baker Book House)
Oxford Bible Atlas, Herbert G. May and G. H. Hunt (Oxford)

9. Bible History
   a. Old Testament History
      A Survey of Israel's History, Leon J. Wood (Zondervan)
      Old Testament Bible History, Alfred Edersheim (Eerdmans)
      Old Testament Times, Roland K. Harrison (Eerdmans)
   b. New Testament History
      New Testament Times, Merrill C. Tenney (Eerdmans)
      New Testament History, F. F. Bruce (Doubleday)
      Joachim Jeremias, *Jerusalem in the Time of Jesus: An Investigation into Economic & Social Conditions During the New Testament Period,* trans. F. A. and C. H. Cave (Fortress)
      A New Testament History: The Story of the Emerging Church, Floyd V. Filson (Westminster)

10. Charts & Chronological Outlines
    Chronological and Background Charts of the New Testament, H. Wayne House (Zondervan)
    Chronological Charts of the Old Testament, John Walton (Zondervan)
    The Student's Chronological New Testament, A. T. Robertson (Fleming H. Revell)

11. Archaeology
    The New International Dictionary of Biblical Archaeology, E. M. Blaiklock and Roland K. Harrison (Zondervan)
    The Bible and Archaeology, J. A. Thompson (Eerdmans)
    Archaeology and the Old Testament, Merrill F. Unger (Zondervan)
    Archaeology and the New Testament, Merrill F. Unger (Zondervan)

12. Commentaries
    a. Whole Bible—Single Volume
       The New Bible Commentary, Donald Guthrie, J. A. Motyer, Alan M. Stibbs, and Donald J. Wiseman (Eerdmans)
       Commentary on the Whole Bible, Robert Jamieson, A. P. Fausset, and David Brown (Zondervan)
    b. Whole Bible—Multiple Volume Sets
       An Exposition of the Old & New Testaments, 6 vols., Matthew Henry (Fleming H. Revell)
       The New American Commentary, 40 vols. (Broadman Press, 1991-)
       Barnes' Notes on the Old & New Testaments, 27 vols., Albert Barnes (Baker)
       Lange's Commentary on the Holy Scriptures, 12 vols., John Peter Lange (Zondervan)
       Calvin's Commentaries, 22 vols., John Calvin (Baker)
       A Commentary on the Holy Bible, 3 vols. Matthew Poole (Banner of Truth)
    c. Old Testament
       The New International Commentary on the Old Testament, 6 vols., ed. Roland K. Harrison (Eerdmans)
       Tyndale Old Testament Commentaries, projected multivolume, ed. Donald J. Weisman (Inter-Varsity)—popular
       Biblical Commentary on the Old Testament, 25 vols., Carl F. Keil and Franz Delitzsch (Eerdmans)—advanced
    d. New Testament
       Meyer's Commentary on the New Testament, 11 vols., H. A. Meyer (BMH Books)
       The New International Commentary on the New Testament, 15 vols., ed. F. F. Bruce (Eerdmans)—advanced
       Tyndale New Testament Commentaries, 20 vols., ed. Randolph V. G. Tasker (Eerdmans)

Interpretation of the New Testament, 14 vols., Charles Henry Lenski (Augsburg); advanced
New International Greek Testament Commentary, ed. I. H. Marshall (Eerdmans)

e. Other Recommendations

The usual recommendation is to obtain a good one-volume commentary on the whole Bible, and then one good set of commentaries on the entire Bible. After that, it usually is better to obtain individual book choices, such as Hodge on Romans, Morgan on Acts, and Spurgeon on the Psalms (*The Treasury of David*). Good authors on individual Bible books include F. L. Godet, William Hendriksen, C. Hodge, Henry A. Ironside, Guy King, J. B. Lightfoot, David M. Loyd-Jones, G. C. Morgan, H. C. F. Moule, J. C. Ryle, and W. Griffith Thomas.

13. Translations/Paraphrases
    a. Translations
       New American Standard Bible (Holman)
       New International Version (Zondervan; Holman)
       American Standard Version (Nelson), still useful in study.
       Williams New Testament (Holman)
       The Modern Language Bible, Berkley Version (Zondervan)
       New Revised Standard Version (Holman)
       Revised Standard Version (Nelson)
       King James Version (Holman, Nelson)
       New King James Version (Nelson)
    b. Paraphrases
       The Living Bible, Kenneth Taylor (Tyndale)
       The New Testament in Modern English, J. B. Phillips (Macmillan)

14. Word-Study
    The Expanded Vine's Expository Dictionary of New Testament Words, W. E. Vine (Fleming H. Revell)
    Holman Bible Dictionary, ed. Trent C. Butler (Holman, 1991)
    Synonyms of the New Testament, R. C. Trench (Eerdmans)
    Synonyms of the Old Testament, Robert B. Girdlestone (Eerdmans)
    An Expository Dictionary of Old Testament Words, W. E. Vine (Revell)
    Word Pictures in the New Testament, 6 vols., A. T. Robertson (Broadman)
    Word Studies in the New Testament, Marvin Vincent (Eerdmans)
    Webster's Dictionary of English words also is helpful in the study of Bible words.

15. Hebrew and Greek Aids
    The use of these tools usually depends upon the student's knowledge of the original languages. Some however, are usable without that knowledge.
    a. Hebrew—Old Testament
       (1) Lexicon
           A Hebrew and English Lexicon of the Old Testament, Francis Brown, S. R. Driver, and Charles A. Briggs (Oxford)
       (2) Wordbook
           Theological Wordbook of the Old Testament, ed. R. Laird Harris, Gleason L. Archer, Jr., and Bruce K. Waltke, 2 vols. (Moody). Student without Hebrew can use this book well by its cross-references with Strong's Concordance.
           Theological Dictionary of the Old Testament, ed. G. Johannes Botterweck and Helmer Ringgren (Eerdmans)
           Nelson's Expository Dictionary of the Old Testament, ed. Merrill Unger and William White, Jr. (Nelson)
       (3) Interlinear
           The NIV Interlinear Hebrew-English Old Testament, 4 vols., projected, ed. John Kohlenberger III (Zondervan)

(4) Concordance
The Englishman's Hebrew and Chaldee Concordance of the Old Testament, George V. Wigram
(Broadman; Baker)
b. Greek—New Testament
(1) Lexicon
A Greek-English Lexicon of the New Testament, Frederick W. Danker and F. Wilbur Gingrich
(Zondervan)
A Reader's Greek-English Lexicon to the New Testament, S. Kubo (Zondervan)
Parsing Guide to the Greek New Testament, E. S. Hans (Herald)
The Analytical Greek Lexicon Revised, ed. H. K. Moulton (Zondervan)
Thayer's Greek-English Lexicon of the New Testament, Joseph H. Thayer (Broadman)
(2) Wordbook
A Theological Dictionary of the New Testament, 9 vols., Gerhard Kittel (Eerdmans)
Dictionary of the New Testament Theology, 3 vols., Colin Brown (Zondervan)
A Linguistic Key to the Greek New Testament, Fritz Reinecker (Zondervan)
(3) Interlinear
Interlinear Greek-English New Testament, George R. Berry (Broadman)
The Interlinear Greek-English New Testament, Alfred Marshall (Zondervan)
(4) Concordance
The Word Study Concordance, George V. Wigram and Ralph D. Winter; Companion volume:
The Word Study New Testament, Ralph D. Winter (Tyndale) These books enable students
without Greek to cross-reference to Kittel's *Dictionary* and Arndt and Gingrich's *Lexicon.*
Concordance to the Greek Testament, W. F. Moulton and A. S. Geden (Kregel Publishers)
(5) Text Critical Analysis
A Textual Commentary on the Greek New Testament, ed. Bruce M. Metzger (United Bible
Societies)

16. Concordance (English)
The values of concordances vary according to their purpose and use.
The Exhaustive Concordance of the Bible, James Strong (Abingdon), is correlated with the
linguistic tools (#15 above) more than any other concordance.
Analytical Concordance to the Bible, Robert Young (Eerdmans).
The NIV Complete Concordance, ed. Edward W. Goodrick and John R. Kohlenberger, III (Zondervan)
New American Standard Exhaustive Concordance of the Bible, Robert L. Thomas (Holman)

17. Cross-References
The Treasury of Scripture Knowledge (MacDonald)
Study Bibles include helpful cross-references also.

18. Harmonies
a. Old Testament
A Synoptic Harmony of Samuel, Kings, and Chronicles, ed. James D. Newsome, Jr. (Baker),
includes related passages from Psalms, Isaiah, Jeremiah, and Ezra
A Harmony of Samuel, Kings, & Chronicles, William D. Crockett (Baker)
b. Gospels
A Harmony of the Gospels (NASB), Robert L. Thomas and Stanley N. Gundry (Moody)
A Layman's Harmony of the Gospels, John F. Carter (Broadman)
Gospel Parallels, B. H. Throckmorton (Nelson)
New Harmony of the Gospels, Albert C. Weiand (Eerdmans)
Synopsis of the Four Gospels: Greek-English Edition, Kurt Aland (United Bible Society)
The Horizontal Line Synopsis of the Gospels, R. J. Swanson (Western NC Press)
c. Paul
A Harmony of the Life of St. Paul, Frank J. Goodwin (Baker)

19. Topical Bible
The New Nave's Topical Bible, Orville J. Nave (Zondervan)
The Zondervan Topical Bible, ed. Edward Viening (Zondervan)

20. Theology
    a. Baptist
       Systematic Theology, 3 vols. in one, Augustus H. Strong (Judson)
       Christian Theology, Millard J. Erickson (Baker) presents a "moderate form" of Calvinism
    b. Calvinist
       Institutes of the Christian Religion, 2 vols., John Calvin (Westminster)
       Systematic Theology of the Christian Religion, J. Oliver Buswell, Jr. (Zondervan); premillennial
       Lectures in Systematic Theology, Henry C. Thiessen (Eerdmans); modified Calvinistic, premillennial
       Systematic Theology, L. Berkhof (Eerdmans); amillennial
       Systematic Theology, 3 vols., Charles Hodge (Eerdmans); postmillennial
    c. Arminian
       Christian Theology, 2 vols., H. O. Wiley (presently out of print)
       A Contemporary Wesleyan Theology, 2 vols., Charles W. Carter (Zondervan)
       God, Man, and Salvation, W. T. Purkiser et al. (Baker)
       Systematics: A Study of the Christian System of Life & Thought, Leroy Forlines (Randall House)
    d. Biblical (showing the historical development of theology derived inductively from the basic biblical texts)
       (1) Old Testament
           Toward an Old Testament Theology, W. C. Kaiser (Zondervan)
           Themes in Old Testament Theology, W. Dryness (Inter-Varsity)
           The Theology of the Older Testament, J. B. Payne (Zondervan)
       (2) New Testament
           New Testament Theology, Donald Guthrie (Inter-Varsity)
           New Testament Theology, Leon Morris (Zondervan)
           A Theology of the New Testament, George E. Ladd (Eerdmans)

Appendix C
How We Got God's Word

General Introduction treats the critical questions about the Bible's integrity, such as inspiration, authority, canon, languages, text, genuineness, authenticity, and credibility.

Process by which God speaks to humans: Revelation, Inspiration, Preservation, and Illumination.

I. Revelation

Definition: self-disclosure of God through some form of divine communication.

A. General Revelation (natural theology)—in nature, history, and conscience (Acts 17:27-29; Rom. 1:18-27; 2:14-15).

B. Special Revelation—truth about God's nature, redemptive acts, purpose, and will for human beings that they could not learn through natural channels.

Special revelation was given through various means (Heb. 1:1-2) until it was bound up in the written Word of God (2 Tim. 3:15-17; 2 Pet. 3:15-16). Special revelation is propositional in nature, that is, it is expressed in declarative sentences. The goal of special revelation is that men and women can know and fellowship with God.

II. Inspiration

Definition: God's supernatural influence that superintended human authors, using their own individual personalities, in composing and recording the message of God to humans, without error in the original manuscripts.

A. Wrong Views
1. Natural—no supernatural inspiration; writers were literary geniuses like Milton and Shakespeare.
2. Mechanical (Dictation, dynamic)—human authors were passive automatons (mouthpieces, or dictaphones) and were insensitive to what they were writing.
3. Partial—Only parts relating to faith and practice are without error.
4. Concept—God gave the general ideas and human authors expressed them in their own fallible words and thus errors crept in.
5. Neoorthodox—a human book that "contains" God's Word and becomes the Word of God to individuals by the present speaking of the Holy Spirit.

B. The Bible that Inspiration Produced
1. Authoritative—sole rule for faith and conduct. All people are under obligation to believe and obey it (John 12:48-50).
2. Inerrant—free from error and not contrary to fact in its statements. Infallible, trustworthy, true in whatever areas it touches (2 Pet. 1:20-21).
3. Plenary, Verbal—all the writings are equally inspired; every word was divinely guided. (Matt. 5:17-18).

C. Evidences of Inspiration
   1. Its Claims—continually asserts that it is of God.
   2. Its Christ—central figure has no parallel in any religion (incarnation, perfect life, miracles, teaching, substitutionary atonement, and ability to transform His followers).
   3. Its Superiority—superior to the teachings of any other book, superlative above all other religions.
   4. Its Peculiar Message—its true, good, and holy God; depravity of mankind; substitutionary atonement of Christ.
   5. Its Moral and Ethical Teaching—made a greater impact upon history than all other books combined; incomparably superior to every other book.
   6. Its Unity—nearly forty different authors, over some sixteen hundred years, forms one harmonious volume, with a progression of thought from beginning to end.
   7. Its Infinity—answers the great questions of life as does no other book.
   8. Its Depths—inexhaustible, infallible truths that transcend our knowledge.
   9. Its Accuracy—supported by archaeological discoveries.
  10. Its Fulfilled Prophecies—minute details, time elements and unlikeliness of fulfillment; pertaining to the nations, Israel, and Jesus Christ.
  11. Its History—always acknowledged by the church to be the Word of God.
  12. Its Indestructibility—most persecuted book, yet stands stronger than ever.
  13. Its Universal Appeal—to all periods of history, all races, classes, and ages.
  14. Its Timelessness—never out of date, continues to be spread over the world.
  15. Its Life-Giving Power—convicting and transforming; has brought salvation, purity, joy, and beauty to untold numbers of persons.
  16. Its Adherents' Character—upright character of those who accept it in contrast to those who reject it.
  17. Its Spirit's Witness—inner witness that convinces the believer of its inspiration and authenticates its truth.

D. The Nature of the Influence by Which Inspiration Was Accomplished
   1. Human Element Seen—God gave His Word in a way that allowed human personality to show. Peculiar styles and mannerisms are clearly traceable in the writings.
   2. Supervised by God—Holy Spirit exercised a supervision that led the writer to write what was needful and to keep his writings free from error (Luke 1:1-4).
   3. Dictation Sometimes—Sometimes God spoke directly and the writer recorded His direct words (Ex. 20:1; Isa. 43:1). But oftentimes the writers were left to choose their own words.
   4. Objective Interjection—Sometimes the writers did not understand the full implications of that which they wrote (Dan. 12:8-9; 1 Pet. 1:10-12).

E. The Canon of Scripture
Definition: The Greek term *kanon* meant "reed," and came to mean a standard "measuring rod" by which things were judged. By the fourth century the word came to be used to designate (a) the rule by which each divinely inspired book of Scripture is tested, and (b) the collection of books that meet the standard.
   1. Completion—In the providence of God, the writings that were stamped with divine authority and bore a self-authenticating character were accepted by the church as normative. The "apocryphal" books were refused a place in the sacred canon by Protestant churches, though accepted by Roman Catholics.
   2. Tests of Canonicity
     a) The tests of canonicity for an Old Testament book appear to be as follows:
       (1) Written by an accredited messenger of God (a prophet)
       (2) Regarded by its recipients as obligatory
       (3) Written in Hebrew (with some Aramaic)
       (4) Harmonized with the Law
       (5) Demonstrated its value by close association with Israel's worship
       (6) Free from contradictions, inaccuracies, inconsistencies, and peculiar practices

b) The tests of canonicity of the New Testament books are as follows:
  (1) Written by an accredited messenger of God (an apostle or a companion of an apostle)
  (2) Read in the churches as a whole and recognized as obligatory
  (3) Recognized and used by the early church fathers
  (4) In agreement with the doctrine, or rule of faith, received orally from the apostles
  (5) Able to edify the Christian reader
  (6) Bears the witness of the Spirit as being inspired of God

III. Preservation

God has preserved His Word through the centuries. We have God's Word today in spite of human efforts to destroy and discount it and in spite of the frailty of human copyists. Christ has declared, "Heaven and earth will pass away, but My words shall not pass away" (Matt. 24:35).

  A. Textual Criticism (the scientific investigation of literary documents to discover their origin, history, or original form) has demonstrated a high degree of accuracy in the transmitted text. Consecrated scholars have searched out scribal errors that may have crept into the transmitted text.

  B. Textual Differences in copies of the Scriptures are few, and they have no serious effect upon the theological accuracy of the Bible we have in hand today.

  C. The Story of English Translations. John Wycliffe (1384) was the first person to translate the entire Bible into English. His translation from the Latin Vulgate was a protest against the evil of his age. It gave impetus to a movement that was the beginning of the reformation in England.

William Tyndale (1530) had been driven out of England. His New Testament in English first appeared at Worms, Germany. He translated from the Greek and Hebrew. His work created such bitter opposition from the papal power that he was burned at the stake. His New Testament was the first to be printed in English. His Bible translation was foundational to subsequent translations.

CHART OF THE ENGLISH BIBLE

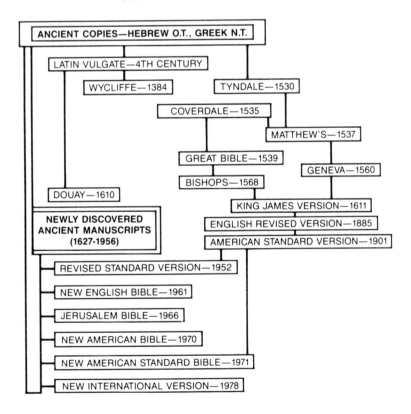

IV. Illumination

Illumination is that activity of the Holy Spirit that makes it possible for persons to receive and understand scriptural truth. It is not the communication to us of new knowledge beyond what is contained in the Bible. It is not a new revelation, but is the giving of spiritual enlightenment concerning the completed revelation of His Word. Christ promised, "But when He, the Spirit of truth, is come, He will guide you into all the truth . . . for He shall take of Mine and shall disclose it to you" (John 16:13-14; See also 1 Cor. 2:12-13).

Appendix D
Variations in the Transmitted Text

The following is an example of how we may deal with the problem of textual variations in the many copies of Scripture that are extant. It is a genealogical tree diagram for the Book of Philippians. Four ancient text-types that have been traced are the Alexandrian, Antiochian, Caesarean, and Western. Different generations of copies, as well as mixtures of copies, are seen in the diagram (the chart does not include all the many random generation copies).

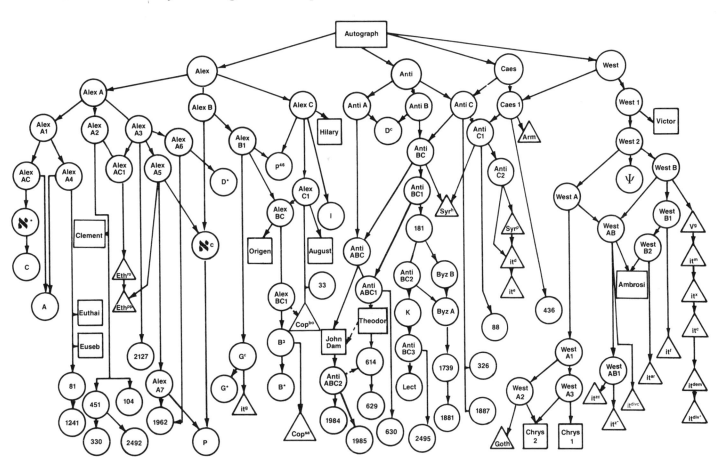

A Typical Problem of Textual Variations

Four different versions of a phrase in Philippians 1:14 have been found in the copies, as follows:
(1) the word of God to speak,
(2) the word to speak,
(3) the word of Lord to speak,
(4) the word to speak of God.
The problem we face is the following question: Which version is the actual text of the original autograph (manuscript)?

Support of the Four Versions

(1) The first version is supported by all Alexandrian copies (except p. 46, D*, and G^c), and by two second-generation branches of Antiochian (anti-A and anti-C), and by Caesarean and all Western. The evidence is strong and distributed with only one weak alternative. This reading is the choice of the *New American Standard Version*, the *New International Version*, and the *Revised Standard Version*.

(2) The second version is supported only by one second generation branch (Anti B), and is best understood as a careless omission. The support is weak and local. This reading is the choice of the *King James Version* and the *New King James Version*.

(3) The third version is supported by only one fourth-generation Alexandrian branch (G^c and its descendants). It probably is a confusion, because G^c contains several other careless blunders.

(4) The fourth version is supported only by D* and its Old Latin companion it^d (with its descendant it^e). Probably this version is caused by a transposition of letters within a word; D* contains several other careless blunders.

Conclusion

Which version (1, 2, 3, or 4) do you believe is the actual text of the original autograph? Why? Viewing the genealogical tree diagram, we find overwhelming support for version number one and very little support for the other three versions. The first version is supported by almost all Alexandrian copies, the Caesarean and Western copies, and two second-generation branches of Antiochian. The other versions are understood as either a careless omission or a careless blunder.

We can agree with the NASB and the NIV in their choice of the first version: "to speak the word of God." (The rearrangement of the Greek phrase "the word of God to speak" to the English phrase "to speak the word of God" is simply a matter of syntax—the way words are put together to form sentences, which varies from one language to another.)

(The information in this appendix is drawn from James D. Price, "A Computer-Aided Textual Commentary of the Book of Philippians," *Grace Theological Journal* 8 [Fall 1987]: 253-90.)

Answers

Chapter 1
A. 1-Christ, 2-soul, 3-God, 4-life; B. 1-mirror (conviction), 2-fire and hammer (breaking), 3-water (cleansing), 4-food (strength and growth), 5-light (guidance), 6-sword (victory), 7-money (spiritual success), 8-seed (fruitful ministry); C. 1-desire, 2-dependence, 3-discipline

Chapter 2
1-D, 2-B, 3-A, 4-E, 5-C, 6-F, 7-general, 8-special, 9-archaeology, 10-topical, 11-Bible survey and book study.

Chapter 3
A-7; B-3; C-9; D-1; E-6; F-2,7; G-2,8,9,11; H-1,2,3,4,6.

Chapter 4
A-16, B-12, C-18, D-14, E-13, F-16, 17, 19, G-at least six of the tools.

Chapter 5
A-3,4,8,10; B-1,5,6,12; C-2,7,9,11.